TOM
KERRIDGE

FRESH START

BLOOMSBURY ABSOLUTE
LONDON · OXFORD · NEW YORK · NEW DELHI · SYDNEY

This book is dedicated to family! Mine and yours.
Bef, Acey and the dogs – love you so much!
To all the Kerridges and all the Cullens,
thank you from the bottom of my heart.

CONTENTS

♡ Vegetarian recipes
❋ Recipes that are good for freezing

Hello you lot...

I love nothing more than seeing people enjoying their food – I love it so much I've made a career from it! As a chef, it gives me a huge amount of satisfaction, as I go home at the end of the night, to know I've contributed to guests at the restaurant having a good time. Cooking and eating together is one of life's great pleasures and, although it sounds a bit cheesy, I truly believe that making a meal to share is one of the best ways to show those around you that you care about them. It strengthen bonds and creates lasting memories.

Despite this, though, a few years ago I was stuck in a rut of bad habits, making poor choices about what, and how much, I consumed. Coupled with a hectic work life and long hours, this was doing me no favours at all. Missing breakfast, choosing high-sugar and high-salt 'pick me ups' during the day and alcohol-absorbing starchy carbs at night, I was massively overweight and had developed a routine of eating convenience food most days. I needed to make a lifestyle change – literally to save my life – and I wanted to be a good example to my young son, Acey. I now make it a real priority to set aside time each week to eat proper home-cooked meals as a family. It may not be every night, but it's as often as we can and I know that it's helping Acey develop a good relationship with food too.

We all know we should be eating less processed food and yet more of us than ever are regularly turning to ready-meals and takeaways instead of cooking from scratch. I get why: we're busy, and convenience food is exactly that – convenient! But relying on it isn't good for us. I want to show you that cooking your own food really isn't as difficult as you might think. OK, so it might take a bit more effort than just bunging a ready-meal in the microwave and waiting for the ping, but your meals will taste so much better, I promise. And there's the added bonus that you will have complete control over what goes into the food you eat.

Eat better, feel better

Although this isn't a 'healthy eating' or 'diet' book, without doubt you'll be encouraging better health for you and your family by cooking more of your own food. If you've got out of the routine of shopping for, and cooking proper meals, it can feel a bit daunting to get started again. Maybe you've fallen into the busy-life trap and after a long day you just don't feel you have the time or energy to spend in the kitchen; or maybe you've never really cooked before and don't know where to begin. Perhaps you just want to try something new, instead of turning to the same handful of dishes you make again and again. That's where the recipes in this book come in. I want you to feel excited about cooking, so they have been designed to help you have fun in the kitchen and maybe even to kick-start a new, healthier you in the process.

I'm not asking you to spend hours whipping up restaurant-style food – good food needn't be time-consuming. Just take it one meal at a time and build up your skills and confidence slowly. If you start out with dishes that use ingredients and flavours you're familiar with, you'll know how they should taste, and then, as your confidence grows, you can experiment more. The Prawn and broccoli rice noodles on page 56 is a good recipe to start out with, as it's both quick and easy. Or maybe you want to make homemade pizzas, chicken curry or a lighter version of bangers and mash? Turn to pages 150, 166 and 86 for these family favourites.

Once you start having control over what ingredients go into the food you cook, you'll find you become more aware of what you eat overall. In this book there are many lower-calorie recipes. I've also included plenty of vegetarian dishes, shown by the ♡ symbol. Actually, there's an entire chapter devoted to easy ways to get more veg into your diet. And as you become increasingly mindful of your food choices, you might well find you're more interested in your health and fitness generally. Maybe you'll even sign up for a 10K run! Personally, I don't recommend obsessing over calorie counting, but I've listed the rough calories per portion on the recipes in case you are keeping an eye on your calorie intake because you have a bit of extra weight to lose.

I'd also encourage you to get all the family involved, whatever 'family' might mean to you – whether that's the kids, your partner or housemates. Cooking and eating is one of the easiest and most pleasurable ways to spend time together, and the benefits go way beyond simply eating higher-quality food. So, instead of staying glued to the TV or phone, make time to prepare a proper meal together and eat it around the table.

Don't get me wrong: I'm not against all convenience food – it fulfils a need for many people. But it should be the exception not the norm. If you start to think convenience food is for every day, then that's what it'll become.

Habits start young for children and I think we should encourage them to have a healthy relationship with food as early as possible, so they grow up open to trying new things and less likely to become fussy eaters. Talk about what you're doing while you're chopping the veg or stirring a pot on the stove. Learn where your food comes from and try new ingredients. Go on a food adventure together! You can sample new flavours from different countries around the world from your own kitchen – how amazing is that?

If you're used to eating a lot of ready meals and packaged foods, home cooking can take some getting used to. It might even take a bit of time for your taste buds to adjust to those great new tastes. Start off with easy swaps: ditch your sugary cereal for the granola on page 28, perhaps, or replace your regular week-night takeaway with one of my curries. Once you realise how good home-cooked food can be, you'll never go back.

Be the boss in your kitchen

The first step towards cooking with confidence is to own your kitchen. Know where everything is and have the essentials within easy reach of the hob, so you're not rummaging around at the back of a drawer or cupboard trying to find the wooden spoon or baking tray you need. Think of the place where you work – your desk, forklift truck, behind the bar. You know that space inside out and even if you're not the official boss, you're in charge. You need to feel the same way about your kitchen. Don't be intimidated by it, make it your zone.

You don't need to buy the fanciest kitchen equipment in order to cook really good food – a couple of decent pans, a sharp knife and chopping board, a mixing bowl, a wooden spoon, a whisk, a roasting tray and a baking tray will do! If you feel like splashing out, then investing in a food processor will save you loads of time chopping and mixing, and it's great for making quick sauces and soups. Also, make sure you have some storage containers for prepping meals in advance, keeping leftovers and freezing meals. You'll easily save the money you spend on these by not buying takeaways!

Now that you've got your workspace in order, start thinking about what you're going to cook. This is the fun bit. These days, many of us often leave the decision-making about what to eat that night until we're on our way home from work and then we'll dash into the supermarket and pick up something quick. But this can lead to some pretty poor choices. People used to work out what they were going to eat each day of the week ahead, and then do a big shop – supplementing it with a few extra fresh ingredients every few days. Let's try and get back into the habit of doing that a bit more, as it saves time and money. Every bit of food you buy will be destined for a meal, so you won't waste food, and you won't be tempted to nip into the chippie as you pass it because you'll have a delicious meal planned at home.

For many people, it's actually time – or rather a lack of it – that is the real barrier to cooking your own meals from scratch. If your work schedule means you're not home until late, I completely understand how something out of a packet, which takes just a few minutes to cook, can seem to tick all the right boxes. My working hours often mean I'm home late, after Acey has gone to bed. But because of that I make the times when I am home early enough for us to all eat as a family really count.

I know it can be tough. When I was growing up my mum worked in the evenings and so from an early age I was cooking for us – and it was fish fingers and waffles because they were easy. But my mum made the weekends matter. On Sundays we'd make a big lunch and she'd get us involved with peeling and prepping the veg, including the sprouts at Christmas. We'd go to pick-your-own fruit farms in the summer and see who could find the largest strawberry, or who could pick the most. These are some of my favourite memories as a child. Even though we weren't able to sit down and eat proper meals together every night of the week, I still grew up with a connection to real food. Don't put yourself under pressure, just do what you can and make it work for you.

This is where we return to forward planning. I'm a big supporter of cooking in big batches and freezing meals for later, so there's a whole chapter devoted to 'batch cooking' in this book. If you have meals stashed in the freezer, all you need to do is defrost one and away you go. Your own supply of convenience food! It's a great way of getting in control of your mealtimes, and means there are no excuses for ordering in. Every now and then, set aside some time for making meals for the freezer – why not try Italian turkey meatballs on page 171 or a takeaway favourite like the Beef biriyani on page 172?

There's also the common misconception that cooking from scratch is expensive. Some ready meals are cheap, but they tend to contain few fresh ingredients and less nutrients than freshly cooked food. I've come up with loads of easy, delicious recipes made with affordable ingredients for you to try. There are other ways to save money on food, too: frozen produce, such as fish, peas and broad beans, can be cheaper than fresh, for example. Batch cooking is a great way to bring down costs as well. In the long run, though, investing in mealtimes now will pay you back in the future – in terms of your family's health. And, as you adjust your approach to food and shopping, you'll find you don't have to spend a lot to eat well.

Enjoy your food

Cooking and eating should be all about enjoyment, so have some fun with it. Don't get hung up about creating restaurant-quality food – behind the scenes in a professional kitchen is a whole team working together! The goal here is to serve up tasty, home-cooked recipes for you and your family, and about spending some proper time together.

I'd like you to treat my recipes more as guidelines than instructions. Maybe I've suggested you use two garlic cloves but if you think you need five, then go for it! Once you've tried out one or two new recipes and mastered a few basic cooking techniques, you'll develop your own preferences and I want you to feel free to experiment with the recipes. Puddings are a little bit different as the ingredients and quantities often play a scientific role, determining whether your cake will rise or your pudding sets, for example. But with stews and casseroles, mince dishes, soups and salads, go ahead and play around

What is the worst that could happen? You'll quickly learn what works well together, and what is less successful, so enjoy the process! You wouldn't just jump on a skateboard and start doing tricks immediately – you have to learn the basics first and probably fall off a few times. It's the same with cooking, but you'll be doing culinary kick-flips before you know it.

So, chuck that pizza delivery menu in the recycling bin, be brave and let's give you and your family a fresh start!

Getting kitchen-comfortable

Cooking regularly from scratch can take a bit of getting used to, so I thought I'd give you some tips and suggestions to help you on your way. Putting together a good store cupboard will really save you time and money, for example, and I'm also sharing a few techniques I use to maximise flavour.

Basic ingredients

Keeping a supply of the basic ingredients you use most often will mean you're only ever moments away from a nutritious meal, even on a busy week night.

Store cupboard

- Pasta, rice, lentils, noodles or quinoa are convenient bases for quick midweek meals. Those ready-cooked pouches of rice and lentils can be brilliant too – a neat little crossover convenience food.

- Tins of tomatoes, coconut milk, beans (such as kidney, borlotti and butterbeans), chickpeas, sweetcorn and tuna are great standbys. I use them regularly in pasta sauces, curries, stews and salads, and for making fish cakes. Jars of passata are also useful for quick sauces.

- Dried herbs and spices lift many dishes, so keep a nice range on the shelf. The dried herbs I use most often are thyme, oregano and bay leaves. Dried herbs are strongly flavoured so you won't need to use as much as fresh herbs. (For more on fresh herbs, see opposite.)

- When it comes to spices, my favourites are fennel, cumin and coriander seeds, chilli flakes, ground turmeric, cumin and coriander, and hot and sweet smoked paprika. I also like cardamom pods, cinnamon and nutmeg, which all bring an exotic warmth to puddings and cakes, as well as savoury dishes. Ready-made spice blends are really great to have in the cupboard too. I like garam masala, Madras curry powder, ras el hanout and Chinese five-spice powder.

- Flaky sea salt and black peppercorns for grinding are essentials, of course – it's so important to properly season your food. Always taste it before you season it, though, so you don't overdo it, especially when preparing food for children. I also use fragrant Szechuan peppercorns in stir-fries.

- Onions, garlic and fresh ginger are always in my cupboard at home. They are versatile and add huge amounts of flavour.

- Olive oil is a must. I suggest keeping a mild olive oil for general cooking and frying, and a good-quality extra-virgin olive oil for making salad dressings. For cooking at high temperatures and for Asian-style dishes, I prefer to use a flavourless oil, like groundnut or vegetable oil. I also keep sesame oil and chilli oil to add a powerful punch to dressings and for drizzling on finished dishes.

- Vinegar, including red and white wine vinegar and sherry vinegar, can provide the much-needed acidity to help balance the overall flavour of a dish. It will enhance other flavours, too. I generally use rice wine vinegar in Asian-style dishes like stir-fries.

- Other high-impact extras that I like to keep around are liquid aminos (which you can find in some supermarkets and online), soy sauce, fish sauce, Worcestershire sauce and Sriracha hot sauce. You don't need a lot of these powerhouse ingredients to make meals taste exciting.

- Honey and maple syrup are great natural sweeteners that I use in both sweet and savoury dishes, from cakes and ice cream to stir-fry sauces.

- Vanilla extract is wonderful for enhancing all sorts of puddings, and also for adding extra flavour to your morning pancakes (page 33). Make sure you buy the real thing, not synthetic vanilla flavouring.

- A selection of nuts and seeds add a healthy crunch to lots of recipes, from pasta bakes to salads and from porridge to loaf cakes. Pistachios, peanuts, coconut flakes, sunflower seeds, black sesame seeds and pumpkin seeds are the ones I use the most. (For more on dry-frying nuts and seeds to bring out their flavours, see page 20.).

Counter-top

- Grow pots of your favourite herbs on your counter top or windowsill so you can snip some off whenever a recipe calls for them. Herbs are great for adding really fresh flavours: flat-leaf parsley, coriander, mint, basil, thyme and oregano are particularly useful. If you buy bunches or bags of fresh herbs instead, keep them in the fridge or in a jug of water.

Fridge standbys

- Have jars of anchovies, olives, capers, peppercorns and sun-dried tomatoes to add pockets of intense flavour to savoury dishes.

- Mustard provides a great flavour kick. I often stir a spoonful through stews to add extra depth, use it in salad dressings or combine some with mayonnaise to spread in a wrap or a sandwich. Mustards vary quite a lot in heat and taste. To cover all needs, keep a Dijon mustard, a hot English mustard and a sweeter, milder one, like American or German.

- Tomato purée and tahini, harissa, curry, chipotle and tamarind pastes are easy ways to add complex layers of flavour to a recipe. These are each used in slightly different ways but achieve the same result of elevating simple ingredients to a rich and exotic finished dish.

Fresh ingredients

- Eggs are something I eat often, not just for breakfast. If you've got eggs in your fridge, you've got a meal, even if it's just a simple omelette with fresh herbs on top. Try to use organic and free-range eggs where you can – they really do taste better. Most of the recipes in this book use large eggs. Bring eggs to room temperature before you use them, especially in baking.

- Meat is an ingredient I'm happy to use less often than I used to, but when I do eat it, I make sure I choose proper good-quality meat. Try to buy the best you can afford, ideally free-range and organic. I mostly use lower-fat mince (5% fat) and leaner cuts at home, trimming off most of the excess fat. Occasionally I will use a higher fat percentage mince (such as 10% fat), as the extra fat can help to bind the other ingredients together. Don't forget to rest cuts of meat after you've cooked them, as this helps to make the meat nice and tender. For larger cuts, shoulder and leg joints, for example, I like to cook them low and slow in the oven, which allows the meat to become really succulent and tender, almost falling off the bone. And roasting meat in this way means you don't have to worry about overcooking your Sunday lunch!

- Yoghurt has a wonderfully cooling and slightly acidic taste, which can instantly balance a dish. You can also add endless flavours to it – from tahini or chilli sauce to fresh herbs, chopped cucumber or capers –

to make a savoury dip, or the base for a salad dressing. And I'll happily have yoghurt for breakfast with some granola or fruit, if I'm in a rush. Its thick and creamy texture is also good for making a quick fruit fool, or a fresh-tasting icing for a cake. I generally use low-fat natural yoghurt or 0% fat Greek-style yoghurt, which has a creamier texture. Sometimes, however, full-fat yoghurt is essential for getting the texture right, for example in the pannacotta on page 220.

- Stock is always best if it's freshly made. It's easy to cook up chicken, fish or vegetable stock yourself at home (it freezes well), and you can also buy it in most supermarkets or butchers. Using it is an easy way to introduce some really great flavour to your cooking. That said, good-quality instant stock cubes will do the job too.

- Lemons, oranges and limes are brilliant for introducing fresh-tasting flavours. Citrus juice is ideal for making simple dressings and brings a sharp tang to sweet and savoury dishes. If you intend to use the zest, buy unwaxed citrus fruit. The zest has a more gentle, complex flavour and is ideal for lifting savoury dishes and flavouring puddings. (See page 20 for how to zest citrus fruit.)

Freezer

- Bags of frozen peas and prawns are endlessly versatile – I use them in everything from stir-fries and pasta dishes to risottos and curries, as well as simple salads and wraps.

- Frozen mixed berries can be blitzed to make smoothies, an effortless compote (page 34) or an instant ice cream (page 226).

- Frozen fish keeps really well and it can often be fresher than what you buy at the fish counter, as it will have been frozen at sea. Salmon, cod or haddock steaks are so easy to cook – just wrap them in foil and cook in the oven, or use them in a one-tray bake (page 210).

Flavour-plus cooking

As well as thinking about the ingredients you use, there are some clever, straightforward cooking techniques that can help enhance the flavour and texture of your food.

Grating garlic You'll see that in most recipes I tend to peel and then finely grate garlic. You could crush or finely slice your garlic instead, but using a fine grater gently squeezes out all the natural oils so you get twice as much flavour from each clove, and the taste is a bit less harsh.

Caramelising onions Compared with regular frying, this is a slow process. You want the onions to cook gently over a really low heat until they start to become sticky, turn golden brown and are so soft they're almost breaking down. To ensure they cook evenly, you'll need to stir them fairly often. They will develop a sweet, almost toffee-ish flavour, which means you don't need to add any extra sweetness later on. In the veggie bolognaise on page 148, the onion is cooked like this, along with some tomato purée. It works sort of like a curry paste, creating complex flavours that provide a solid base for the rest of the sauce.

Pre-roasting mince Browning mince in the oven, before you introduce it to the rest of your recipe, allows the outside to caramelise, adding an extra, subtle sweetness and richness to the final dish. Pre-cooking mince in this way has the added bonus of cooking off some of the fat, making it healthier too.

Toasting nuts and seeds Gently toasting or 'dry-frying' nuts and seeds enhances their flavour. Use a small non-stick pan over a medium heat, swirling the pan every now and then until they start to smell delicious and turn golden brown. ('Dry-frying' just means without any oil.) I add toasted nuts and seeds to salads or scatter them over the top of almost anything else for a lovely layer of tasty crunch. To add flavour to oats for making porridge (page 30) and the flapjacks on page 247, I toast the oats in the oven first.

Julienning vegetables Preparing vegetable 'julienne' is basically just cutting them into evenly sized matchsticks. If you are cooking veg prepared like this, the uniform size helps them to cook evenly.

Zesting citrus fruit Buy unwaxed fruit and use a fine grater to remove the zest, making sure you don't get any of the bitter white pith underneath. Grating the zest releases all the lovely citrusy oils.

Cooking pasta Always add salt to the boiling water before cooking pasta. This is the only opportunity the pasta gets to be properly seasoned. And be careful not to overcook your pasta either – no one likes it mushy! Carefully lift a piece from the pan and try it. It should be *al dente*: softened, but still with a little 'bite' or firmness.

Blowtorching This may sound a bit cheffy, but a cook's blowtorch won't cost you much and it's a great way of adding a smoky, barbecued flavour to dishes, or to create a caramelised or charred effect without having to use lots of oil. To use a blowtorch safely, don't touch the flame and always check the gas has been switched off afterwards. Place the food on a metal tray and make sure there is nothing flammable nearby, like alcohol. Always light the blowtorch before putting it near raw food, or you run the risk of getting fuel on the food. I find that the best technique is to use a gentle waving motion, so the flame goes slowly back and forth across the surface of the food to evenly 'scorch' it. Don't concentrate too long on one area, or the food may burn. I use this method on the trout with beetroot and orange on page 106. Trout is a delicate fish that you would struggle to barbecue conventionally, so this allows you to introduce all those delicious flavours without the risk of it getting stuck to your grill. Blowtorching also adds an amazing caramelised flavour to the Orange, cardamom and polenta cake on page 252.

Making friends with your oven

Ovens vary more than you'd think. If you turn the dial on your oven to 180°C you might actually find it's up to 20°C hotter or cooler than it should be – and it's generally hotter near the top than the bottom as that's where the heating element usually is. In some recipes I specify that you should use the top shelf (best for browning) or bottom shelf (when slow cooking, for example). It's a good idea to get an oven thermometer, so you can work out exactly what temperature your oven is cooking at, and whether that varies, top to bottom.

Most ovens these days can be operated as either fan or conventional ovens. Using the fan means the heat is circulated throughout the oven more evenly. The fan oven setting is more often used, but if you're an experienced cook you might prefer to cook cakes and delicate meringues using the conventional option, as the fan-assisted heat can cause them to dry out or cook too quickly on the outside before they've had a chance to cook properly inside. Sophisticated ovens can have even more options to choose from, such as using top or bottom heat with or without a fan, and most ovens now have an integral grill.

Freezing extra food

If lack of time is holding you back from making home-cooked meals, get your freezer to work hard for you. Many of the recipes in this book are particularly well suited to freezing and reheating later, and I've given instructions for how to go about it wherever you see this symbol: ❄

Invest in some good-quality freezable containers – two-person portion sizes are very useful, as well as re-usable freezer bags. A range of rigid plastic or glass containers, and foil trays with cardboard or foil lids, are great for freezing your own meals.

Make sure you let your food cool properly before you freeze it. If you don't, it can partially defrost the other food in your freezer and force your freezer to work twice as hard. And don't forget to label and date the contents!

When you want to eat something from the freezer, defrost it fully in the fridge overnight before reheating it in the oven (or on the hob) until it's piping hot all the way through.

Relax and have fun

One of the best ways of enjoying food is to share it with others. So invite your mates round, get the conversation flowing and serve up some simple tasty food for everyone to dig into. Don't get stressed about it, or worry about how you're going to present your food – it doesn't have to be perfect. Set big sharing platters in the middle of the table and let everyone help themselves. If it's a lasagne or tray bake, I'll often put the baking dish directly on the table (on a heat mat) with some serving spoons, rather than plate up everything individually. Just sit back and enjoy!

MORNINGS CAN OFTEN feel quite rushed. If you need to get to work early and/or you have children to get ready for school, then I totally understand how a quick bowl of cereal or slice of toast often seems like the most you can manage. But if you set aside a little time in your regular morning routine for some proper food, you'll be getting a head start on the rest of the day.

When you're in a tearing hurry, attempting to cook something new for breakfast might seem like too much of a challenge, so try out a few recipes at the weekend first and then, when you're familiar with them, start introducing them on weekdays. For the mornings when you really do only have 5 minutes (and we all have those) keep a jar of the granola from page 28 at the ready. It's full of nutty, fruity goodness and has to be better for you than sugary, salty, highly processed cereal from a packet.

To avoid the mid-morning slump and help keep you fuller for longer, eggs are a fantastic breakfast ingredient because they're packed with protein. The Indian-style scrambled eggs on page 44 are quick and filling, and they've got green beans in the mix too, so you'll also be getting one of your five-a-day. Veg at breakfast time might sound a bit odd, but the beans provide a lovely, satisfying crunch that contrasts with the creamy, fluffy eggs. Or, for a nice alternative to a boiled egg, my Smoked haddock and spinach egg pots (page 38) are perfect for dipping toast into. And if you're after a treat at the weekend, Eggy brioche with berry compote on page 34 will get everyone into the kitchen to see what's cooking!

It's not all about eggs though – if you can't do without your morning bacon, then try the BLT on page 40; I guarantee it will be the best BLT you'll ever eat. With all this choice, there really are no excuses for missing out on the most important meal of the day.

Homemade granola

Packed with nutritious nuts and dried fruit, this granola is a great way to start the day, and it's a healthier alternative to the highly processed, high-sugar cereals you can buy. It is really sustaining too, so you only need a small amount, with a generous dollop of yoghurt and some fresh fruit, for a perfectly balanced breakfast. ∨

16 servings
240 calories per serving

300g rolled oats
100g mixed seeds (pumpkin,
 sunflower and sesame)
50g hazelnuts, roughly chopped
50g pecans, roughly chopped
50g pistachios, roughly chopped
50g flaked almonds
4 tbsp coconut oil
125ml maple syrup
50ml honey
2 tbsp vanilla extract
½ tsp ground cardamom
½ tsp ground ginger
1 tsp ground cinnamon
1 tsp sea salt flakes
50g coconut flakes
150g mixed dried fruit (cranberries,
 chopped apricots, chopped
 dried apple, raisins)

To serve
Fresh fruit
Yoghurt

1 Preheat the oven to 170°C/Fan 150°C/Gas 3. Line two baking trays with baking parchment.

2 Mix the oats, seeds, chopped nuts and flaked almonds together in a large bowl.

3 Put the coconut oil, maple syrup, honey, vanilla and spices into a small saucepan and heat gently, stirring, until the coconut oil has melted. Pour over the oat mixture, add the salt and mix well.

4 Spread the mixture out in a thin layer on the prepared trays and bake for 15 minutes. Remove from the oven and add the coconut flakes and dried fruit. Mix well, then bake for a further 8–10 minutes or until the coconut flakes are browned. Remove from the oven and set aside to cool.

5 Store the granola in an airtight container. Serve with fresh fruit and yoghurt.

Pimp my porridge

Porridge is very good for you, but if you find it a bit bland, try one of my tasty toppings. For a fruity option, go for the fresh raspberry and nut, or spiced pear with dates and almonds. Porridge doesn't have to be sweet, though, so if you can't do without bacon and eggs in the morning, give my savoury option a go.

Serves 2
270–430 calories per serving (depending on the type of milk used and chosen topping)

For the porridge base
100g rolled oats
800ml water
270ml milk (whole milk, coconut or almond)

For the raspberry and nut topping
100g raspberries
3 tbsp coconut sugar
2 tbsp pistachios, chopped

For the spiced pear topping
30g butter
3 tbsp soft light brown sugar
1 tsp ground mixed spice
2 pears, cored and diced
3 tbsp water
8 dates, chopped
2 tbsp almonds, toasted

For the bacon and egg topping
100g bacon lardons
1 tsp light olive oil
2 tbsp maple syrup
2 large free-range eggs
Sea salt
Barbecue sauce, to serve (optional)

1 For the porridge base, preheat the oven to 200°C/Fan 180°C/Gas 6 and line a baking tray with baking parchment. Spread the oats out on the tray and toast on the top shelf of the oven for 10 minutes or until golden brown. Transfer the oats to a large non-stick saucepan, add the water and milk and simmer gently for 4–5 minutes, stirring occasionally, as it thickens.

2 For the raspberry and nut topping, mix half of the raspberries and coconut sugar into the porridge base and divide between two bowls. Top with the remaining raspberries, sugar and the pistachios.

3 Or for the spiced pear topping, melt the butter in a small saucepan over a medium heat. Add the sugar, spice, pears and water. Stir, then cook for 4–5 minutes. Add the dates and cook for a further 2 minutes. Ladle the porridge into two bowls and spoon the pear mix on top. Sprinkle with the toasted almonds to serve.

4 Or for the bacon and egg topping, cook the lardons in the olive oil in a small non-stick frying pan over a medium-high heat until well browned and super crispy, about 10–12 minutes. Tip the lardons into a small bowl and add the maple syrup. Return the pan to the heat, adding a little more oil if needed. Crack the eggs into the pan and cook sunny side up for 2–3 minutes, until the whites are set and the yolks are still runny. Add a little salt to the porridge base and ladle into two bowls. Top each portion with a fried egg and the lardons. Add a little barbecue sauce too, if you fancy it.

Nutty wholemeal pancakes

Extra toasty nuttiness from the wholemeal flour and nutty banana topping makes these easy pancakes even tastier than the classic white flour version – and they're better for you too. ♡

Serves 4
675 calories per serving

300g wholemeal self-raising flour
1 tsp baking powder
½ tsp ground cinnamon
½ tsp ground mixed spice
A pinch of sea salt
2 large free-range eggs
300ml whole or semi-skimmed milk
2 tbsp nut butter
3 tbsp light brown sugar
1 tbsp vanilla extract
4 bananas, sliced
40g pecans, toasted and finely
     chopped
40g peanuts, toasted and finely
     chopped
Vegetable oil, for cooking
Maple syrup, to serve

1 Preheat the oven to 140°C/Fan 120°C/Gas 1.

2 Put the flour, baking powder, spices and salt into a large bowl. Crack the eggs and separate the yolks into one bowl and the whites into another very clean medium bowl.

3 Add the milk, nut butter, sugar and vanilla extract to the egg yolks and mix well.

4 In a small bowl, mash one of the bananas to a pulp and then add to the flour mix, along with half the chopped nuts. Pour in the milk and egg yolk mixture and whisk to a thick, smooth batter.

5 Beat the egg whites with an electric hand whisk until soft peaks form. Fold half of the egg whites into the batter until just combined, then fold in the rest.

6 Heat a little oil in a large non-stick frying pan over a medium heat. You will need to cook the pancakes in batches. When the pan is hot, add 2 or 3 ladlefuls of the mixture to the pan, keeping them separate. Cook for 2–3 minutes until bubbles start to appear on the surface, then flip the pancakes over and cook for 2–3 minutes on the other side. Transfer to a baking tray and keep warm in the oven. Repeat with the rest of the batter.

7 Place two pancakes on each warmed plate and top with the sliced bananas, the rest of the chopped nuts and a trickle of maple syrup.

Eggy brioche with berry compote

This is a fun weekend breakfast to get the kids involved in – mixing the eggs and dunking the bread. Make sure you use big doorstop slices of brioche. You'll have twice as much compote as you need here but it will keep in the fridge for a few days and is delicious dolloped on yoghurt or porridge. ♥

Serves 4
535 calories per serving

For the berry compote
2 Granny Smith apples
75g light brown sugar
Juice of ½ lemon
¼ tsp ground mixed spice
1 tbsp water
300g frozen mixed berries

For the eggy brioche
3 large free-range eggs
200ml whole or semi-skimmed milk
½ tsp ground cinnamon
1 tbsp vanilla extract
4 slices of brioche, 4cm thick
30g butter
30g icing sugar

1 Preheat the oven to 150°C/Fan 130°C/Gas 2.

2 For the compote, peel, quarter, core and dice the apples. Place them in a medium saucepan with the brown sugar, lemon juice, mixed spice and water over a medium-low heat. Cook gently for 5 minutes, then add the frozen berries, bring to a gentle simmer and cook for a further 8–10 minutes or until the liquor is reduced and slightly thickened.

3 Meanwhile, for the eggy brioche, crack the eggs into a shallow bowl. Add the milk, cinnamon and vanilla extract and whisk until combined. Dip 2 brioche slices into the beaten egg mix, until well soaked.

4 Melt half the butter in a large non-stick frying pan over a medium-high heat. When bubbling, add the soaked brioche and cook for 2–3 minutes on each side until golden. Remove from the pan and transfer to an oven tray. Keep warm in the oven while you dip and fry the rest of the brioche, using the remaining butter.

5 Sprinkle one side of each brioche slice liberally with icing sugar and caramelise, using a cook's blowtorch. Serve the caramelised brioche slices with the warm berry compote.

Corn cakes with Mexican beans

These corn cakes are made from an easy batter, with beaten egg whites to make them really light and fluffy. Alongside the warmly spiced Mexican beans, they make a relaxed breakfast-meets-lunch dish. ♡

Serves 4
515 calories per serving

For the Mexican beans
1 tbsp vegetable oil
1 red onion, finely chopped
2 garlic cloves, finely chopped
1 tsp ground cumin
1 tsp sweet smoked paprika
400g tin chopped tomatoes
400g tin kidney beans, rinsed and drained
100ml water
Sea salt and freshly ground black pepper

For the corn cakes
340g tinned sweetcorn kernels, drained (285g drained weight)
4 spring onions, thinly sliced
75g mature Cheddar, grated
100g self-raising flour
50g cornflour
2 large free-range eggs
80ml whole or semi-skimmed milk
1-2 tbsp olive oil, for frying

To serve
1 ripe avocado, peeled, stoned, quartered and sliced
1 lime, cut into 4 wedges
A handful of coriander

1 For the beans, heat the oil in a sauté pan over a medium heat. Add the onion and cook for 2 minutes, then add the garlic and stir for 1 minute. Sprinkle in the spices, stir for a minute, then add the tinned tomatoes, kidney beans and water. Simmer gently for about 15 minutes, until slightly reduced and thickened.

2 Meanwhile, for the corn cakes, preheat the oven to 140°C/Fan 120°C/Gas 1. Put the sweetcorn kernels, spring onions, cheese, flour, cornflour and a little salt and pepper into a bowl and mix well to combine.

3 Crack the eggs and separate the yolks into one bowl and the whites into another very clean medium bowl. Add the milk to the egg yolks and beat well, then pour into the corn mixture and mix until well combined. Using an electric hand whisk, whisk the egg whites to soft peaks, then gently fold into the corn mixture.

4 You'll need to cook the corn cakes in batches. Heat a little oil in a non-stick frying pan over a medium-high heat. When hot, drop 3 or 4 tablespoonfuls of the mixture into the pan, placing them well apart. Cook for 2–3 minutes until bubbles appear on the surface, then flip the corn cakes over and cook for 2–3 minutes on the other side. Transfer to a baking tray; keep warm in the oven while you cook the rest of the batter, adding more oil as necessary, to make about 20 cakes in total.

5 Just before serving, gently reheat the beans. Serve the corn cakes with the Mexican beans, avocado slices, lime wedges and fresh coriander.

Smoked haddock and spinach egg pots

Baked eggs are becoming quite fashionable for breakfast and these are packed with flavour from the smoked haddock, cheese and spinach. They puff up beautifully in the oven and are great for scooping up with slices of buttered rye bread.

Serves 4
390 calories per serving

1 tsp softened butter, for greasing
4 tbsp fresh breadcrumbs
**200g undyed skinless smoked
    haddock fillets**
200g baby spinach
2 tbsp water
6 large free-range eggs
200ml crème fraîche
¼ tsp freshly grated nutmeg
50g Cheddar, grated
**Sweet smoked paprika, for
    sprinkling**
**Sea salt and freshly ground black
    pepper**
Chopped flat-leaf parsley, to finish
**Rye toast soldiers, buttered,
    to serve**

1 Preheat the oven to 200°C/Fan 180°C/Gas 6. Butter the insides of four 250ml ramekins or cocotte dishes, then dust with breadcrumbs.

2 Check the smoked haddock for any pin-bones, then cut into dice and divide between the dishes. Stand the dishes on a baking tray.

3 Put the spinach into a large pan with the water. Place over a high heat and stir until the spinach has wilted, about 3–4 minutes. Remove from the heat and drain in a colander. Leave to cool slightly, then squeeze out as much liquid from the spinach as possible. Chop roughly and divide between the 4 baking dishes.

4 Whisk the eggs and crème fraîche together in a bowl and season with the grated nutmeg and a little salt and pepper. Pour the egg mixture into the dishes and sprinkle the grated cheese and a little smoked paprika over the surface.

5 Place the tray on the middle shelf of the oven and bake for 10 minutes. Turn the oven to the grill setting (medium-high). Cook the egg pots for a further 5 minutes or until the cheese is golden brown.

6 Sprinkle with chopped parsley and serve with buttered rye toast soldiers on the side.

Tom's BLT

This is the best BLT you'll ever eat! A bold claim, I know, but it has so much going on in terms of creaminess from the avocado, crispy, salty bacon and a crunchy acidity from the fried capers that cuts through the richness.

Serves 4
655 calories per serving

8 rashers of smoked streaky bacon
1 red onion, cut into 4 thick slices
80g lardons
1 beef tomato, cut into 4 even slices
2 ripe avocados
Juice of ½ lime
A handful of coriander, roughly
**   chopped**
Sriracha hot sauce, to taste
4 large free-range eggs
2 tbsp capers, drained
Sea salt and freshly ground black
**   pepper**

To assemble
4 wholemeal baps, halved and
**   toasted**
2 tbsp mayonnaise
1 Little Gem lettuce, leaves
**   separated**

1 Preheat the oven to 220°C/Fan 200°C/Gas 7. Line two baking trays with baking parchment.

2 Lay the bacon rashers and red onion slices out on the lined trays and cook in the oven for 15–20 minutes or until the bacon is browned and crispy.

3 Meanwhile, cook the lardons in a medium non-stick frying pan over a medium-high heat until crispy, about 10–12 minutes. Remove from the pan and set aside. Sprinkle the beef tomato slices with a little salt.

4 Halve and stone the avocados, scrape the flesh out of the skins into a bowl and mash roughly. Add the lime juice and coriander and mix well to make a guacamole. Season with hot sauce, salt and pepper to taste, then stir through the crispy lardons.

5 Return the empty lardon pan to the heat. When hot, crack in the eggs and cook them sunny side up for 2–3 minutes until the whites are just set and the yolks are still runny. Sprinkle in the capers and allow them to crisp up a little. Season the eggs with a little pepper.

6 Lay the toasted bun bases on serving plates, spread with a little mayonnaise and top with the guacamole, lettuce and tomato slices. Add a couple of slices of streaky bacon and top with the fried egg, some capers and a roasted onion slice. Sandwich together with the bun tops and serve.

Ham and potato hash with poached eggs

This is a cross between the ultimate hash brown and a rösti. It takes a little while to get the potatoes nice and crispy so it's maybe one to save for the weekend, but you can get ahead and make the mash the day before if you like.

Serves 4
545 calories per serving

1kg potatoes, peeled and cut into 5cm pieces
1 tbsp vegetable oil
30g butter
1 red onion, finely chopped
1 green pepper, cored, deseeded and diced
200g smoked ham, diced
4 sprigs of thyme, leaves picked
1 tbsp German mustard
½ tsp cayenne pepper
40g Parmesan, finely grated
4 large free-range eggs
2 tbsp flat-leaf parsley, finely chopped
1 ripe avocado, quartered and sliced
16 cherry tomatoes, halved
Sea salt and freshly ground black pepper

1 Cook the potatoes in boiling salted water for about 10 minutes, until tender. Drain them well and crush lightly, then set aside.

2 Heat the oil and butter in a large non-stick frying pan over a high heat. Add the onion and cook until browned. Add the green pepper and ham and cook for about 10 minutes until the pepper is softened. Remove from the heat.

3 In a bowl, mix together the crushed potatoes, onion, pepper and ham mix, thyme, mustard and cayenne.

4 Sprinkle half the grated Parmesan over the bottom of the frying pan. Place over a medium heat and add the potato mixture, spreading it out in an even layer. Scatter over the remaining Parmesan. Cook, without moving, for 10 minutes or until crispy on the underside.

5 Now turn the potato mixture over. Cook for a further 10 minutes, or until crispy on the other side and hot all the way through. You may want to flip it over again for a few minutes.

6 Meanwhile, poach the eggs in a large shallow pan of simmering salted water for 3–4 minutes. Carefully remove with a slotted spoon, drain on kitchen paper and set aside.

7 Scatter the chopped parsley on top of the hash. Divide between warmed plates and place a poached egg on each portion. Serve the avocado slices and cherry tomatoes alongside.

Indian-style scrambled eggs

Eggs are great for breakfast any day of the week, as they are packed with protein and nutrients. These lightly spiced scrambled eggs make a fantastic alternative to the classic version and they also get you a head start on your five-a-day. ♡

Serves 4
580 calories per serving

1 tbsp vegetable oil
1 tbsp yellow mustard seeds
1 tsp cumin seeds
1 onion, finely chopped
2 garlic cloves, finely chopped
2.5cm piece of fresh ginger, grated
1 green pepper, cored, deseeded and finely diced
300g green beans, finely sliced
A handful of curry leaves, finely chopped
1–2 long green chillies, sliced (optional)
2 tsp hot Madras curry powder
8 large free-range eggs
150ml single cream
50g butter
A handful of coriander, roughly chopped
Sea salt and freshly ground black pepper
Thick sourdough toast, buttered, to serve

1 Heat the oil in a large non-stick frying pan over a high heat, then add the mustard and cumin seeds. Once they are sizzling, add the onion and sauté for 3–4 minutes, until softened. Add the garlic and ginger and cook for another 2 minutes.

2 Add the green pepper, green beans, curry leaves and green chilli(es), if using, and cook for 2 minutes. Lower the heat to medium, stir in the curry powder and cook for 1 minute, until fragrant.

3 In a bowl, beat the eggs with the cream and season well with salt and pepper.

4 Add the butter to the frying pan, and once melted, gently fold through the beaten egg mix. Cook, stirring lightly a few times, until the eggs are almost cooked through but still slightly runny in places.

5 Toss through the shredded coriander and serve on warmed plates, with buttered toasted sourdough.

TIP ✔ This would also work well using Mexican spices, such as paprika, chipotle and chilli flakes instead of the mustard seeds and curry powder.

Smoked salmon and scrambled egg muffins with asparagus

Smoked salmon and scrambled eggs is a luxurious combination and the asparagus adds a satisfying fresh crunch to it. Duck eggs are richer than hen's eggs and this is a great way to enjoy them, but you can use free-range hen's eggs if you prefer. This is an easy one to double or triple up for a weekend brunch with friends – just put it all on big plates in the middle of the table so everyone can help themselves.

Serves 2
705 calories per serving

4 free-range duck eggs
1-2 tbsp finely chopped chives
2 tbsp butter
100ml crème fraîche
100g smoked salmon
Sea salt and freshly ground black pepper

For the asparagus
120g asparagus spears, trimmed
1 tbsp butter
3 tbsp water

To serve
2 large English muffins, freshly toasted, split and buttered

1 Crack the eggs into a bowl, add half of the chives with a little salt and pepper and whisk together.

2 To cook the asparagus, put the asparagus spears into a small saucepan with the butter, water and a little salt and pepper. Place over a high heat and allow the butter to melt, then cook for 4–5 minutes or until the liquor reduces down to a glaze.

3 Meanwhile, to cook the scrambled eggs, place a non-stick frying pan over a medium-low heat and add the butter. Once it has melted, add the beaten eggs and cook over a low heat for 4–5 minutes, stirring gently a few times, until the egg is just starting to set. Take the pan off the heat and mix in the crème fraîche.

4 Place a toasted muffin on each warmed plate and pile the soft scrambled eggs on top. Wipe the frying pan clean and place over a high heat. When the pan is hot, add the smoked salmon for just a few seconds to warm through, until it just changes colour.

5 Lay the smoked salmon on top of the scrambled eggs and sprinkle with the remaining chives. Add the glazed asparagus to the plates, grind over a little pepper and serve.

Scrambled tofu

This effortless breakfast dish is packed with veg for a healthy and colourful start to your day. Tofu is a great alternative to scrambled eggs and it has a satisfying texture when cooked properly. ♡

Serves 4
340 calories per serving

1 tbsp olive oil
1 red onion, diced
1 red pepper, cored, deseeded and diced
1 yellow pepper, cored, deseeded and diced
1 courgette, diced
8 mushrooms, thickly sliced
1 tsp ground turmeric
450g smoked tofu
2 tbsp butter
3 handfuls of baby spinach
2 tbsp liquid aminos
Sea salt and freshly ground black pepper
Multigrain toast, buttered, to serve

1 Heat the olive oil in a non-stick frying pan. Add the onion and sauté for 3–4 minutes, then toss in the peppers and cook for a further 4 minutes.

2 Add the courgette and mushrooms to the pan and cook for 2–3 minutes until slightly softened.

3 Sprinkle in the turmeric and roughly crumble the tofu into the pan. Add the butter, stir well and cook until gently warmed through. If it seems a little dry, add a dash of water.

4 Stir through the spinach and liquid aminos and cook briefly, until the spinach wilts. Taste and adjust the seasoning, adding salt and pepper as needed.

5 Serve the scrambled tofu on warmed plates, with buttered toast.

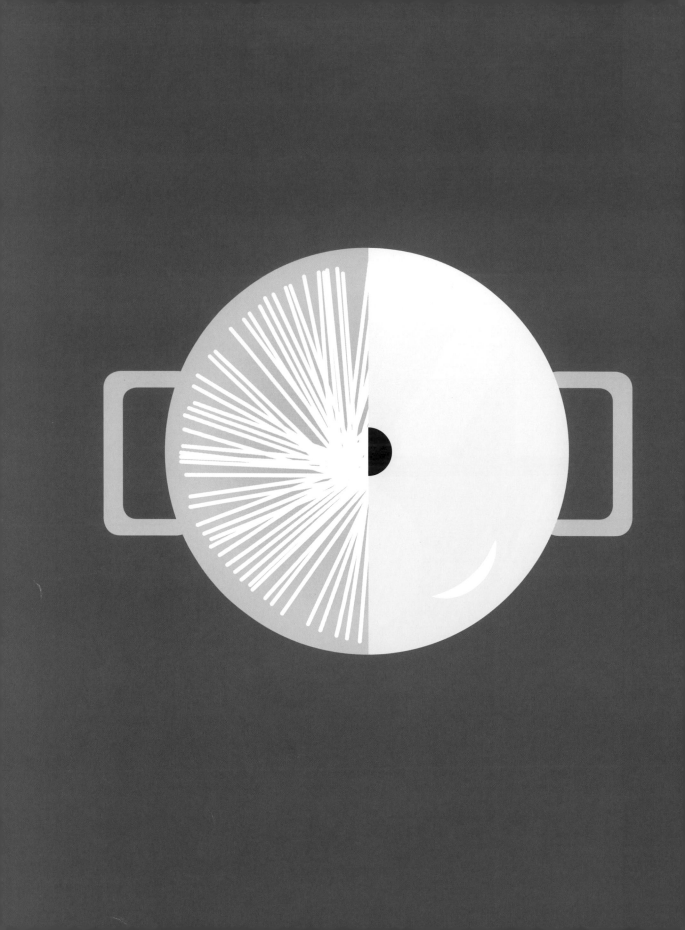

BEING SHORT ON TIME doesn't mean your food needs to be short on flavour, or that you take shortcuts with your health either. The recipes in this chapter are designed for those busy weekdays when you might be more inclined to order a takeaway or pick up a ready-meal on your way home.

So that you have all your ingredients to hand when you need them, plan out what you're going to eat over the next few days then do a big shop. And try to keep your cupboard stocked with the basics too, then you'll only ever be minutes away from a tasty meal, even if you haven't had time to shop.

Ingredients like pasta and noodles are great to have on standby for when you want something quick. If you regularly eat your pasta with a jar of ready-made sauce stirred through it, then try the tasty puttanesca sauce on page 64 or the smoked salmon and peppercorn medley on page 60 instead. Both of these easy sauces rely on just a few high-flavour ingredients from the store cupboard, such as a jar of olives or tin of tomatoes. Instant flavour-boosts like these – as well as spices, fresh chilli and garlic – are key when you don't have much time.

If you're lacking a bit of confidence in the kitchen, start by cooking meals you're familiar with, so you know how they taste. Perhaps try a homemade version of your go-to takeaway, or a dish you're used to buying ready-made. The Turkey schnitzel with green slaw on page 72 is a tasty alternative to breaded chicken, or try the Peanut chicken stir-fry noodles on page 68, which has a satay-style sauce. For a really easy recipe, the tomato salad on page 89 involves almost no cooking at all, just chopping tomatoes, griddling chorizo and tossing everything in a powerful dressing.

Midweek cooking should be low-stress and high-flavour – there's no need to cook a fancy meal every night. As these recipes show, if you use quality ingredients and simple techniques, you can't go wrong.

Crab mayo on griddled sourdough

This is basically just a fancy open sandwich with layers of crisp, fresh ingredients piled on top of a thick slice of griddled sourdough bread. Of course, you can create your own version using your favourite toppings – just be sure to include a bit of crunch and to balance the flavours with a little sharp acidity.

Serves 4
505 calories per serving

6 rashers of smoked streaky bacon, halved
1 sourdough loaf
1 tbsp olive oil
12 asparagus spears, trimmed
1 tbsp butter
100ml water
1 ripe avocado, thickly sliced
Sea salt and freshly ground black pepper

For the pickled radish
16 radishes, thinly sliced
25g caster sugar
4 tbsp white wine vinegar

For the crab mayo
75g brown crab meat
75g reduced-fat crème fraîche
75g reduced-fat mayonnaise
A squeeze of lemon juice, to taste
300g white crab meat

To serve (optional)
Tabasco

1 Preheat the oven to 220°C/Fan 200°C/Gas 7. Line a baking tray with baking parchment.

2 For the pickled radish, mix the ingredients together in a bowl and leave to pickle.

3 Lay the bacon on the baking tray and place in the oven for 15 minutes, or until crispy.

4 Meanwhile, cut 4 long slices from the middle of the sourdough loaf, each 1cm thick. Preheat a griddle. Brush both sides of the sourdough slices lightly with olive oil and cook on the hot griddle until lightly charred on each side.

5 Place the asparagus in a small frying pan with the butter, water and some salt and pepper. Cook over a medium-high heat for 3–4 minutes or until tender and all the liquid has evaporated.

6 Meanwhile, for the crab mayo, mix together the brown crab meat, crème fraîche, mayonnaise and lemon juice. Season with salt and pepper to taste and gently fold through the white crab meat.

7 Lay each piece of griddled sourdough on a plate. Spread with crab mayo, then top with 3 pieces of bacon, 3 pieces of asparagus and a couple of slices of avocado. Drain the radish from its pickling juices and scatter over the top. If you like things spicy, add a little Tabasco before you tuck in!

Prawn and broccoli rice noodles

If you're feeling unsure about getting into the kitchen, give this fail-safe stir-fry a go. It's full of familiar flavours and is on the table in under half an hour.

Serves 4
475 calories per serving

300g flat rice noodles

For the sauce
2 tbsp fish sauce
2 tbsp soy sauce
2 tbsp tamarind paste
2 tbsp light brown sugar
2 tsp Sriracha hot sauce
150ml water

For the stir-fry
2 tbsp groundnut oil
3 garlic cloves, finely chopped
350g raw tiger prawns, peeled and deveined, leaving the tail shell on
2 long shallots, halved and finely sliced
250g broccoli florets
1 tbsp sesame oil
3 large free-range eggs, lightly beaten
4 spring onions, cut into 2.5cm lengths
2 handfuls of beansprouts
2 tbsp roasted peanuts, lightly crushed, plus extra to finish

To serve
1 long red chilli, finely sliced
1 lime, cut into 4 wedges

1 Add the rice noodles to a bowl of just-boiled water and leave to soak for 10 minutes. Meanwhile, to make the sauce, mix all the ingredients together in a bowl; set aside. Drain the rice noodles in a colander and put to one side.

2 Heat half the groundnut oil in a large wok over a very high heat. When hot, add the garlic and stir-fry for a few seconds. Toss in the prawns and stir-fry for 1–2 minutes until they have turned pink. Remove the wok from the heat and spoon the prawns and garlic out onto a plate. Wipe out the wok with kitchen paper.

3 Put the wok back over a high heat and add the remaining groundnut oil. When hot, toss in the shallots and stir-fry for 2 minutes. Add the broccoli florets and stir-fry for a further 2 minutes. Add the noodles and sauce to the wok and cook, stirring, for 2–3 minutes until the noodles soften.

4 Push the noodles to one side of the pan and add the sesame oil to the other side. Crack the eggs onto the oil and mix around lightly with a wooden spoon. Allow to cook for a minute or two, then stir the eggs around and mix them with the shallots and broccoli.

5 Add the spring onions, beansprouts and peanuts to the wok. Stir fry for 1–2 minutes, then return the prawns to the wok and stir-fry for a minute or two until warmed through.

6 Divide the stir-fry between warmed bowls and top with the sliced chilli and a few roasted peanuts. Serve at once, with lime wedges to squeeze over.

Thai red curry mussels

Thai takeaway curries are often high in salt, sugars and unhealthy fats. This light alternative is made with fresh mussels, which are low in fat. They're also surprisingly inexpensive and steam in no time. Don't be afraid to cook with seafood – all it takes is a little confidence.

Serves 4
560 calories per serving
660 calories with bread

2kg fresh mussels in shells
2 tbsp vegetable oil
2 long shallots, finely sliced
4 garlic cloves, finely sliced
5cm piece of fresh ginger,
finely chopped
3 tbsp Thai red curry paste
400ml coconut milk
1 tbsp fish sauce
1 tbsp oyster sauce
1 tsp caster sugar
2 lime leaves
200g courgettes, diced

To serve
A handful of Thai basil leaves,
roughly chopped
A handful of coriander, roughly
chopped
2 long red chillies, finely sliced
3 spring onions, finely sliced
1 lime, cut into 4 wedges
Crusty bread (optional)

1 Clean the mussels under cold running water, removing any hairy beards and scrubbing off any barnacles. Throw away any open mussels that do not close when tapped sharply on your work surface.

2 Heat the oil in a large, deep sauté pan or a wok (one that has a tight-fitting lid) over a high heat. Add the shallots and cook for 1–2 minutes, then toss in the garlic and ginger and stir-fry for 30 seconds. Stir in the curry paste and cook, stirring, for 30 seconds or until fragrant.

3 Pour in the coconut milk and add the fish sauce, oyster sauce, sugar and lime leaves. Allow to simmer gently for 5 minutes, then add the diced courgettes and cook for a further 2 minutes, stirring often.

4 Tip the cleaned mussels into the pan and stir well to combine with the sauce. Put the lid on and cook over a medium-high heat for 5 minutes or until the shells have opened; discard any that remain closed.

5 Scoop the mussels into warmed serving bowls, making sure you include all the tasty sauce. Scatter over the Thai basil, coriander, chillies and spring onions. Serve straight away, with lime wedges to squeeze over. I like to have crusty bread on the side to soak up all the fantastic flavours.

Smoked salmon and peppercorn pasta

The flavours in this luxurious pasta sauce are quite sophisticated but most of the ingredients can be kept in your store cupboard or fridge, so it's a great convenience meal. The alcohol cooks off in the sauce, but you can leave out the vodka if you prefer.

Serves 4
585 calories per serving

3 tbsp olive oil
2 tbsp capers, drained
1 large red onion, finely chopped
1 fennel bulb, tough outer layer removed, finely diced
3 garlic cloves, finely sliced
1 tbsp green peppercorn in brine, drained
1 tsp pink peppercorns, plus extra to garnish
80ml vodka
2 x 400g tins chopped tomatoes
150ml whipping cream
500g dried casareccia (or fusilli or farfalle) pasta
200g smoked salmon, cut into strips
A handful of flat-leaf parsley, finely chopped
A handful of dill, finely chopped
Sea salt and freshly ground black pepper
1 lemon, cut into wedges, to serve

1 Heat the olive oil a large saucepan over a high heat. Dry the capers well on kitchen paper. When the oil is hot, add the capers and fry for 30 seconds – 1 minute or until they crisp up. Remove from the pan with a slotted spoon and drain on kitchen paper.

2 Lower the heat to medium, add the red onion and fennel to the pan and sauté for 5–7 minutes or until softened. Add the garlic along with the green and pink peppercorns and cook for 2 minutes. Add the vodka and allow to bubble and reduce by half. Stir in the tinned tomatoes and simmer gently for 10 minutes. Stir in the cream and simmer for a further 5 minutes.

3 Meanwhile, bring a large pan of salted water to the boil. Add the pasta and cook until *al dente*, then drain, keeping back a few ladlefuls of the cooking water.

4 Add the smoked salmon to the sauce and mix gently to combine. Add the pasta and a little of the pasta cooking water to create a creamy sauce. Season with salt and black pepper to taste.

5 Divide between warmed serving bowls and sprinkle with a few more pink peppercorns. Scatter over the chopped herbs and serve at once, with lemon wedges to squeeze over.

Italian-style tuna and fennel wraps

Wraps are such a brilliant lunch to take with you on the go. Try these and then experiment with your own favourite filling combinations. You can also buy flavoured wraps – herb, sun-dried tomato or spinach – as well as wholemeal and corn tortillas.

Serves 4
525 calories per serving

2 x 220g jars tuna in olive oil (150g each drained weight)
2 tbsp baby capers, drained
1 small red onion, finely diced
60g pitted black olives, roughly chopped
12 basil leaves, finely chopped
80g reduced-fat mayonnaise
1 small fennel bulb, tough outer layer removed, finely shredded (about 150g)
150g white cabbage, finely shredded
Juice of 1 lemon
4 large tortillas
120g cherry tomatoes, halved
1 ripe avocado, quartered and thickly sliced
Sea salt and freshly ground black pepper

1 Drain the tuna of its oil and place in a large bowl. Add the capers, red onion, olives, chopped basil and mayonnaise. Season with salt and pepper and mix well, breaking up the tuna as you do so.

2 Put the shredded fennel and cabbage into another large bowl. Add the lemon juice and season with salt and pepper. Toss to mix.

3 Lay the tortillas on your work surface and divide the tuna mix between them, spooning it down the middle. Top with the fennel and cabbage slaw, cherry tomatoes and avocado.

4 Wrap each tortilla tightly around the filling. Cut the tortillas in half on an angle to serve.

Spaghetti puttanesca

Famously made from leftovers, this sauce is full of fresh, clean flavours and tastes so much better than anything you'll get from a jar. Everything except the tomatoes can be kept to hand in your store cupboard, making this an excellent midweek supper. The garlic ciabatta is a lush extra; leave it out for a lighter meal.

Serves 4
440 calories per serving
605 calories with garlic ciabatta

3 tbsp extra-virgin olive oil
1 red onion, finely chopped
6 garlic cloves, finely sliced
½–1 tsp dried chilli flakes
12 anchovy fillets in oil, drained and roughly chopped
2 tbsp baby capers, drained
100g pitted black olives, sliced
800g cherry tomatoes (600g halved, 200g quartered)
500g dried spaghetti
A handful of flat-leaf parsley, finely chopped
Sea salt and freshly ground black pepper

For the garlic ciabatta (optional)
2 tbsp butter, softened
2 large garlic cloves, finely grated
1 tbsp flat-leaf parsley, finely chopped
30g Parmesan, finely grated
1 ready-to-bake ciabatta, cut into 12 thick slices

To serve
Freshly grated Parmesan

1 If serving garlic ciabatta, prepare it first. Preheat the oven to 200°C/Fan 180°C/Gas 6. Line a baking tray with baking parchment.

2 In a small bowl, mix the butter, garlic, parsley and Parmesan together and add some salt and pepper. Lay the ciabatta slices on the baking tray and spread liberally with the garlic butter. Place on the top shelf of the oven for 12–14 minutes, until golden brown.

3 Meanwhile, heat the extra-virgin oil in a large non-stick sauté pan over a medium heat. Add the red onion and cook for 5–8 minutes, until softened. Add the garlic, chilli flakes and anchovies to the onion and cook for 2–3 minutes. Add the capers, olives and halved cherry tomatoes and cook for 8 minutes until the tomatoes start to soften and break down slightly. Add a small ladleful of pasta water to create a sauce.

4 While the sauce is cooking, bring a large pan of salted water to the boil. Add the spaghetti and cook for 2 minutes less than the suggested time on the packet, stirring a few times.

5 Drain the spaghetti as soon as it is ready, keeping back a little of the water, and add it to the sauce with the quartered cherry tomatoes and a splash of pasta water. Cook for 3–4 minutes, then stir in the parsley. Season with pepper, and salt if needed (the anchovies will be salty). Serve the pasta in warmed bowls, with Parmesan, and the garlic ciabatta if serving.

Smoky chicken quesadillas

Ideal for getting kids into cooking, these Mexican-style cheesy quesadillas make a great change from fajitas. Have fun getting everyone to add their own toppings and pile on the grated cheese before you cook them in the oven.

Serves 4
835 calories per serving
850 calories with jalapeños

400g cooked chicken, shredded
1 tsp coriander seeds
1 tsp cumin seeds
200g drained, tinned red kidney beans, rinsed
4 spring onions, chopped
200g tin sweetcorn, drained
3 tbsp chipotle paste
8 medium flour tortillas
Olive oil spray (or a little olive oil)
125g reduced-fat mozzarella, grated
125g reduced-fat Cheddar, grated
Sea salt and freshly ground black pepper

For the side salad
2 Little Gem lettuces, leaves separated and halved
70g rocket leaves
100g cherry tomatoes, halved
Juice of ½ lime
2 tbsp extra-virgin olive oil

To finish
Light soured cream
Coriander leaves
Fresh green jalapeños, sliced (optional)
Pickled jalapeños, sliced (optional)

1 Preheat the oven to 220°C/Fan 200°C/Gas 7. Line two baking trays with baking parchment.

2 Put the shredded chicken into a bowl. Heat a small frying pan over a high heat, then add the coriander and cumin seeds and toast for 30 seconds – 1 minute until fragrant. Remove from the heat. Using a pestle and mortar, crush the seeds, then sprinkle over the shredded chicken and toss to coat the pieces.

3 Tip the kidney beans into a bowl and mash lightly with a fork. Add the spring onions, sweetcorn, chipotle paste and a little salt and pepper. Mix well.

4 Place 2 tortillas on each of the lined baking trays. Spray or brush them with a little oil and flip each tortilla over. Spread the kidney bean mixture evenly over the 4 tortillas, top with the chicken and sprinkle with the grated cheeses. Top each one with another tortilla, press down well and spray the surface with a few sprays of oil (or brush with oil if you prefer). Cook in the oven for 10–12 minutes or until the cheese is melted and the tortillas are golden brown.

5 Meanwhile, for the salad, toss the lettuce, rocket and tomatoes together with the lime juice, extra-virgin oil and some salt and pepper.

6 Remove the quesadillas from the oven, cut into wedges and pile onto a plate. Finish with a dollop of soured cream, coriander leaves and sliced jalapeños if you like it spicy. Serve the salad alongside.

Peanut chicken stir-fry noodles

There is so much texture in this easy chicken stir-fry, and flavours everyone knows and loves. The peanuts and cucumber provide a satisfying crunch, and the sweet satay-style sauce is balanced by a final flash of heat from the chilli dressing.

Serves 4
890 calories per serving

**750g fresh or frozen udon noodles
(3 x 250g pouches)**
2 tbsp vegetable oil
**3 large skinless, boneless chicken
breasts, thinly sliced**
**½ tsp Szechuan peppercorns,
crushed**
2 carrots, peeled and julienned
200g mangetout
1 tsp sesame oil
**4 spring onions, finely sliced on
an angle**

For the peanut sauce
3 tbsp crunchy peanut butter
2 tbsp tahini
3 tbsp soy sauce
3 garlic cloves, grated
2.5cm piece of fresh ginger, grated
2 tbsp honey
1 tbsp Sriracha hot sauce
1 tbsp rice wine vinegar
3 tbsp water

For the chilli dressing
100g caster sugar
50ml red wine vinegar
1 tbsp chilli oil
2 tbsp mint leaves, finely chopped

To finish
**50g roasted peanuts, roughly
chopped**
½ cucumber, julienned

1 For the peanut sauce, mix all the ingredients together in a bowl until evenly combined; set aside.

2 Bring a pan of salted water to the boil. Add the noodles, bring back to a simmer and cook until tender, 1–2 minutes. Drain in a colander, keeping back some of the cooking water. Cool the noodles under cold running water and set aside.

3 For the chilli dressing, in a small pan, dissolve the sugar in the wine vinegar over a low heat, stirring often. Increase the heat, bring to the boil, and simmer for 3–4 minutes. Take off the heat and stir in the chilli oil. Let cool completely, then stir in the chopped mint.

4 Heat 1 tbsp of the oil in a large non-stick wok over a high heat until smoking. Add half the chicken, with half the Szechuan peppercorns, and stir-fry for 2 minutes or until it is browned all over and just cooked. Remove and set aside on a plate. Repeat with the remaining chicken and peppercorns (but don't use any more oil).

5 Once all the chicken is cooked and set aside on a plate, add the remaining oil to the wok and return to a high heat. When it is smoking, add the carrots, mangetout and sesame oil and stir-fry for 1 minute.

6 Add the spring onions, noodles, peanut sauce and chicken to the wok, along with a few tablespoonfuls of the reserved noodle cooking water, and stir-fry for 3–4 minutes. Add half the peanuts and mix well. Serve in warmed bowls, topped with more peanuts, cucumber julienne and a drizzle of chilli dressing.

Asian-style glazed chicken thighs

This is a great way to cook succulent chicken thighs. The sweet and sticky Asian glaze is off-set by the quickly pickled cucumber, and using ready-cooked wild rice makes this a really easy midweek supper.

Serves 4
720 calories per serving

8 skinless bone-in chicken thighs

For the Asian glaze
4 tbsp soy sauce
4 tbsp rice wine vinegar
4 tbsp honey
2 tbsp sesame oil
4 garlic cloves, grated
2.5cm piece of fresh ginger, finely grated
½ tsp dried chilli flakes
1 tsp Chinese five-spice powder

For the cucumber pickle
1 cucumber, very thinly sliced
5 tbsp rice wine vinegar
1½ tbsp golden caster sugar

To serve
2 x 250g pouches ready-cooked wild rice mix
2 spring onions, finely sliced
A small handful of toasted sesame seeds
Steamed tenderstem broccoli

1 Preheat the oven to 220°C/Fan 200°C/Gas 7.

2 For the Asian glaze, mix all the ingredients together in a small bowl.

3 Pour the glaze into a small oven dish, lay the chicken thighs in the dish and turn them to coat all over in the glaze. Cook on the middle shelf of the oven for 20–25 minutes (the chicken won't be completely cooked at this stage).

4 Meanwhile, for the cucumber pickle, combine the ingredients in a small bowl and stir until the sugar has dissolved. Set aside.

5 Take the dish out of the oven and spoon the glaze evenly over the chicken thighs. Return to the oven for 10–15 minutes until the chicken is cooked through. Meanwhile, heat up the pouches of rice mix, following the packet instructions.

6 Transfer the glazed chicken to warmed plates and scatter over the spring onions and sesame seeds. Drain the cucumber pickle and divide between the plates. Serve with the rice and tenderstem broccoli.

Turkey schnitzel with green slaw

This is like a giant chicken nugget! So, if your kids only want to eat nuggets, then here is your chance to make your own. The crunchy slaw includes soured cream for a little sharpness, which works well with the richness of schnitzels. You could also try making the slaw with carrots, fennel or even thin slices of apple in place of kale and spinach.

Serves 4
555 calories per serving

4 thin turkey breast escalopes, about 120g each
2 large free-range eggs
60ml milk
150g brown breadcrumbs
30g Parmesan, finely grated
30g white sesame seeds
2 tbsp flat-leaf parsley, finely chopped
3 tbsp light olive oil
Sea salt and freshly ground black pepper

For the green slaw
½ white cabbage, finely shredded
40g kale, stems removed, finely shredded
40g spinach, finely sliced
2 tbsp flat-leaf parsley, finely chopped
4 tbsp mayonnaise
3 tbsp soured cream
1 tsp Dijon mustard
1 tbsp white wine vinegar

To serve
Lemon wedges

1 Preheat the oven to 150°C/Fan 130°C/Gas 2.

2 Season both sides of the turkey escalopes with salt and pepper. In a shallow dish, lightly beat the eggs with the milk. In another dish, mix the brown breadcrumbs with the grated Parmesan, sesame seeds, chopped parsley and a little seasoning.

3 Dip the turkey breast escalopes, one at a time, into the beaten egg, then into the breadcrumb mixture to coat all over.

4 To make the slaw, toss the cabbage, kale, spinach and chopped parsley together in a large bowl. For the dressing, mix the mayonnaise, soured cream, mustard and wine vinegar together in a bowl and season with salt and pepper, then add to the shredded veg and toss to mix; set aside.

5 Heat 2 tbsp of the oil in a large non-stick frying pan over a medium-high heat. When it is hot, add two of the escalopes and fry for 2–3 minutes on each side until golden. Remove and drain on kitchen paper, then transfer to a baking tray and place in the oven to keep warm. Heat the remaining 1 tbsp oil in the pan and cook the other escalopes in the same way.

6 Serve the turkey schnitzel straight away, with the green slaw and lemon wedges to squeeze over.

Five-spiced duck salad

The punchy Asian flavours in this fresh-tasting salad cut through the richness of the duck . Cooking duck breasts is quite different from cooking chicken breasts, as they have a layer of fat, which you want to render out slowly so the skin crisps up nicely. You could use chicken breasts instead of duck here, but be careful not to overcook them as they are lean and can easily dry out.

Serves 4
435 calories per serving

1 tbsp sea salt
1 tsp Chinese five-spice powder
4 duck breasts, skin on

For the salad
100g watercress, any tough stems removed
2 Little Gem lettuces, trimmed, leaves separated
½ cucumber, halved and sliced on an angle
12 radishes, thinly sliced
1 long red chilli, deseeded and thinly sliced
2 handfuls of beansprouts
4 ripe plums or peaches, stoned and cut into slim wedges

For the dressing
3 tbsp hoisin sauce
1 tbsp light soy sauce
2 tsp runny honey
1 tbsp rice wine vinegar
1 tbsp light olive oil
1 tsp sesame oil
Juice of ½ lime

To finish
Mint and coriander leaves

1 Preheat the oven to 200°C/Fan 180°C/Gas 6.

2 Mix the salt and Chinese five-spice powder together in a small bowl. Pat the duck skin dry with kitchen paper, then score with a sharp knife and rub with the spiced salt.

3 Place the duck breasts skin side down in a large ovenproof frying pan, then place the cold pan over a medium-low heat. Cook for 10–15 minutes, or until the skin is golden and crisp. Spoon away some of the fat that is released.

4 Meanwhile, for the salad, mix all the ingredients together in a large bowl.

5 For the dressing, whisk all the ingredients together in a bowl until well combined.

6 Once the duck skin is golden brown and crisp, transfer the pan to the oven for 3–4 minutes to finish the cooking. Remove the duck from the pan and set aside to rest on a warm plate while you dress the salad with the dressing.

7 Divide the salad between serving plates and scatter with mint and coriander leaves. Carve the duck into thick slices and lay on top of the salad. Serve at once.

Crispy beef and pak choi noodles

Ginger and beef is one of my favourite flavour pairings and I love it in this healthier spin on the popular takeaway 'crispy beef'. Pak choi has an amazing crunchy texture, which adds freshness, while the pickled radishes introduce a gentle acidity to balance this colourful noodle dish.

Serves 4
710 calories per serving

For the crispy beef
400g beef topside, thinly sliced
    into strips
½ tsp Szechuan peppercorns,
    crushed
2 tbsp light soy sauce
3 tbsp vegetable or groundnut oil
6 tbsp cornflour

For the quick pickled radish
16 radishes, thinly sliced
2 tsp golden caster sugar
4 tbsp rice wine vinegar

For the stir-fry
5cm piece of fresh ginger, julienned
3 garlic cloves, sliced
4 spring onions, cut into 2.5cm
    lengths
2 long red chillies, sliced on an angle
½ tsp Szechuan peppercorns, lightly
    crushed
700g pak choi, leaves and stems
    separated, both roughly chopped
600g straight-to-wok egg noodles
4 tbsp Shaoxing rice wine
2 tbsp dark soy sauce
1 tbsp light soy sauce
1 tbsp sesame oil
3 tbsp water
100g shelled edamame beans
150g beansprouts

To finish
1 tbsp black sesame seeds

1 In a bowl, toss the beef strips with the Szechuan pepper and soy sauce and leave to marinate for 10 minutes.

2 Meanwhile, for the pickle, put the sliced radishes into a bowl with the sugar and rice wine vinegar. Mix well and set aside.

3 Heat 1 tbsp of the vegetable or groundnut oil in a large wok over a high heat until the oil is smoking. Add the cornflour to the beef and toss to mix.

4 Add one-third of the beef to the wok and stir-fry for 2 minutes, until crispy. Remove with a slotted spoon and set aside on a plate. Repeat with the rest of the beef, using the remaining oil, transferring each batch to the plate once it is cooked.

5 Add the ginger and garlic to the oil left in the wok (from cooking the beef) and stir-fry for 1 minute. Add the spring onions, red chillies, Szechuan pepper and pak choi stems and stir-fry for 2–3 minutes.

6 Add the egg noodles to the wok with the Shaoxing wine, both soy sauces, sesame oil and water. Stir-fry for 2–3 minutes and then add the pak choi leaves, edamame beans and beansprouts. Stir-fry for another 2 minutes until everything is cooked.

7 Serve in warmed bowls, topped with the crispy beef, pickled radishes and sesame seeds.

Rib-eye with broccoli and salsa verde

Cooking steak can feel daunting but at some point you just have to jump off and give it a go! With the griddled broccoli and amazing herby flavours from the salsa verde, this is a lovely, hearty summertime meal – and you definitely won't miss the chips!

Serves 2
1085 calories per serving

2 rib-eye steaks, about 200g each
300g new potatoes, halved
1 tbsp vegetable oil
150g tenderstem broccoli
Sea salt and freshly ground black
   pepper

For the salsa verde
1 long green chilli
1 small garlic clove, peeled
A large handful of parsley leaves
A large handful of basil leaves
A large handful of sage leaves
A large handful of oregano leaves
½ shallot, roughly chopped
½ tsp sweet smoked paprika
4 salted anchovy fillets
1 tsp Dijon mustard
1 tbsp red wine vinegar
80ml extra-virgin olive oil

1 Take the steaks out of the fridge 30 minutes before cooking to bring them to room temperature.

2 Place the potatoes in a pan of boiling salted water. Bring to a simmer and cook for 10–12 minutes or until tender. Drain and keep warm.

3 Meanwhile, heat a large griddle pan over a high heat. Drizzle the steaks, along with the chilli and garlic for the salsa verde, with the oil and season with salt and pepper. Place them all on the hot griddle.

4 Cook the steaks for about 2 minutes on each side for medium-rare steak (allow an extra minute or two if you like it more well done). The chilli and garlic will take around the same time.

5 Transfer the steaks to a plate, cover loosely with foil and rest for a few minutes. Remove the seeds from the chilli, then roughly chop the chilli and garlic.

6 While the steaks are resting, lay the tenderstem broccoli on the griddle and cook for 3–5 minutes, turning frequently, until tender and lightly charred.

7 Meanwhile, put all the ingredients for the salsa verde, including the chopped garlic and chilli, in a food processor. Pulse to a chunky salsa, seasoning with salt and pepper to taste.

8 Slice the steaks and place on warmed plates with the potatoes and broccoli. Spoon on the salsa verde, making sure you cover the potatoes. Serve at once, with a salad on the side if you like.

Spiced lamb cutlets with Bombay aloo

Lamb cutlets are perfect for a week-night supper as they cook in no time, and they work really well with this gently spiced marinade. The Bombay aloo is a flexible side dish that is also good cold, as a twist on a classic potato salad.

Serves 4
645 calories per serving
675 calories with minted yoghurt

12 lamb cutlets
2 tbsp garam masala
Juice of ½ lemon
1 tbsp vegetable oil
Sea salt and freshly ground black pepper

For the Bombay aloo
500g new potatoes
1 tbsp vegetable oil
1 onion, finely chopped
2 garlic cloves, finely chopped
1½ tsp ground coriander
1 tsp cumin seeds
½ tsp ground turmeric
1 tsp ground cumin
½ tsp chilli powder
400g tin chopped tomatoes
250ml water
A handful of coriander, finely chopped

For the minted yoghurt (optional)
A handful of mint leaves
150g Greek yoghurt (0% fat)

1 For the aloo, add the potatoes to a pan of boiling salted water and cook for 12–15 minutes, until tender.

2 Meanwhile, season the lamb cutlets with salt and pepper and place them in a bowl. Add the garam masala, lemon juice and oil, turn the cutlets to coat in the spicy mix and set aside to marinate.

3 Drain the potatoes, halve them and set aside. Heat the oil in a saucepan over a medium-high heat. Add the onion and sauté for 5–10 minutes, until softened. Add the garlic and cook for 2 minutes. Lower the heat, sprinkle in the spices and stir for 30 seconds, then add the tomatoes and 150ml of the water. Bring to a simmer, add some salt and pepper and simmer gently for 10–15 minutes until slightly thickened.

4 Meanwhile, heat a griddle over a medium-high heat. When hot, cook the lamb cutlets on the griddle in 2 or 3 batches for 3–4 minutes on each side, depending on their thickness. Remove to a warm plate and leave to rest under foil for a few minutes.

5 Meanwhile, for the minted yoghurt, if serving, blitz the mint and yoghurt in a small food processor until smooth. Season to taste with salt.

6 Add the potatoes to the tomato sauce along with the remaining 100ml water. Bring to a simmer and simmer for 5 minutes. Stir through the coriander and taste to check the seasoning. Serve the lamb cutlets with the Bombay aloo, and minted yoghurt if serving.

Pork chops with peperonata

Everyone loves a pork chop and the peperonata served alongside brings a real freshness of flavour. It's also an easy way of helping you reach your five-a-day.

Serves 4
740 calories per serving

2 tbsp olive oil
2 onions, thinly sliced
4 garlic cloves, thinly sliced
4 peppers (mixed colours), cored, deseeded and cut into 1cm thick strips
4 thick bone-in, skin-on pork chops, about 250g each
½ tsp smoked paprika
2 tbsp tomato purée
1 tsp paprika
2 large ripe tomatoes, diced
200ml water
Sea salt and freshly ground black pepper
300g green beans, steamed, to serve

1 Heat 1 tbsp olive oil in a large non-stick sauté pan (one with a lid) over a medium-high heat. Add the onions and cook, stirring frequently, for 5 minutes until starting to soften. Add the garlic and peppers, cover and cook for 10 minutes, stirring occasionally.

2 Meanwhile, heat a large non-stick frying pan over a high heat and add the remaining 1 tbsp olive oil. Season the pork chops on both sides with salt, pepper and smoked paprika. Stand the chops in the pan, with the skin edge down, and fry for 5–8 minutes, or until the skin crackles and is crispy (use tongs to hold them if necessary).

3 Add the tomato purée to the peppers and onions and cook for 2–3 minutes, then stir in the paprika and cook for 1 minute. Add the diced tomatoes and pour in the water. Cook, uncovered, for 15–20 minutes, until the peppers are softened. Season with salt and pepper to taste.

4 Once the skin has crisped, cook the pork chops for about 3–4 minutes on each side. Transfer the chops to a warmed plate to rest for a few minutes.

5 Serve the pork chops with the peperonata and steamed green beans.

Chorizo and broccoli stalk pasta

Don't throw away the stalks when you trim broccoli heads. The stalks are also full of flavour and have a satisfying crunch, so just cut off the really woody bits right at the end. Avoiding waste is satisfying, and makes for a cost-effective recipe.

Serves 4
555 calories per serving

500g dried orecchiette (or penne or fusilli) pasta
1 tbsp olive oil
4 cooking chorizo sausages, about 65g each, finely chopped
3 garlic cloves, finely chopped
400g broccoli stalks (about 4), quartered lengthways and finely sliced
3 anchovy fillets in oil, drained and chopped
1 long red chilli, finely chopped
A handful of basil leaves, finely chopped
40g Parmesan, finely grated
Sea salt and freshly ground black pepper
1 lemon, for zesting, to finish

1 Bring a large pan of salted water to the boil. Add the pasta, stir well and cook until *al dente*, about 10–12 minutes.

2 Meanwhile, heat the olive oil in a large non-stick sauté pan over a high heat. When hot, add the chopped chorizo and cook for 4 minutes or until it releases its oil and starts to turn crispy. Add the garlic and cook for 1 minute.

3 Add the sliced broccoli stalks to the pan along with the anchovies and chilli. Cook for a further 3–4 minutes or until the broccoli stalks are just *al dente*.

4 Drain the pasta as soon as it is cooked, saving some of the water. Add the pasta to the chorizo and broccoli pan with a ladleful of the pasta water and stir to make a sauce. Sprinkle in half the chopped basil and half the Parmesan and season with salt and pepper to taste.

5 Toss well and divide between warmed serving bowls. Zest lemon over each bowl and sprinkle with the remaining Parmesan and basil to serve.

Bangers and mash

My version of this ever-popular family favourite uses sweet potato and swede – for variety and extra goodness – to create a mash with an amazing colour. Make sure you use really good-quality sausages as they're the hero of this dish.

Serves 4
705 calories per serving

8 good-quality pork sausages
500g swede, peeled and diced
500g sweet potato, peeled and diced
50g butter
100g half-fat crème fraîche
Sea salt and freshly ground black pepper

For the gravy
1 tbsp olive oil
2 onions, thinly sliced
6 sprigs of thyme, tied together with string
150ml beer (or use an extra 150ml beef stock)
2 tsp English mustard
500ml beef stock
2 tbsp beef gravy granules

To serve
300g green beans, steamed

1 Preheat the oven to 200°C/Fan 180°C/Gas 6. Line a baking tray with baking parchment.

2 Place the sausages on the lined baking tray and cook in the oven for 25–30 minutes, depending on their thickness, shaking the tray from time to time to ensure even cooking.

3 Meanwhile, put the swede and sweet potato into a large pan and pour on enough cold water to cover. Season with salt and bring to the boil. Lower the heat and simmer for 15–20 minutes or until tender.

4 In the meantime, make the gravy. Heat the olive oil in a large non-stick frying pan over a medium-high heat. Add the onions, along with the thyme, and cook, stirring frequently, for 10 minutes or until softened and starting to brown and caramelise.

5 Pour in the beer, if using, and let it reduce by half, then add the mustard and beef stock. Simmer for 10 minutes, then whisk in the gravy granules and stir until thickened. Season with salt and pepper to taste.

6 When the swede and sweet potato are cooked, drain and mash until smooth. Return them to the pan and mix in the butter and crème fraîche. Season with salt and pepper and reheat gently.

7 Serve the sausages with the mash, steamed green beans and plenty of gravy.

Tomato salad with chargrilled chorizo

This effortless dish involves virtually no cooking but is full of flavour and looks stunning. Enjoy it in the summer months when tomatoes are at their best. Source some really good heritage varieties – maybe visit your local farmers' market, or go to a pick-your-own farm – unless, of course, you grow your own!

Serves 4
630 calories per serving

200g sourdough bread, torn into small chunks
5 tbsp extra-virgin olive oil
1kg ripe mixed heritage tomatoes
A pinch of caster sugar
1 small red onion, thinly sliced
1 tbsp baby capers, drained
6 artichokes in brine, drained and quartered
2 handfuls of flat-leaf parsley, leaves picked (10g)
2 tbsp sherry vinegar
4 picante/spicy cooking chorizo sausages, about 300g in total
Sea salt and freshly ground black pepper

1 Preheat the oven to 200°C/Fan 180°C/Gas 6. Line a baking tray with baking parchment.

2 Place the bread on the lined baking tray, drizzle with 1 tbsp of the extra-virgin oil and sprinkle with salt and pepper. Bake in the oven for 10–15 minutes or until browned, tossing once halfway through cooking.

3 Meanwhile, cut the tomatoes into even-sized chunks and place in a large bowl along with the sugar, red onion, capers, artichokes, parsley, sherry vinegar and the remaining 4 tbsp extra-virgin olive oil. Season generously with salt and pepper and toss everything together well.

4 Heat a griddle pan over a medium heat. Slice the chorizo thinly on an angle. Lay the chorizo slices on the hot griddle and cook for 2 minutes on each side. (You might have to do this in batches, depending on the size of your pan.)

5 Add the toasted bread chunks to the tomatoes and toss to coat in the dressing and tomato juices. Add the griddled chorizo and toss again.

6 Transfer the salad to a large, shallow serving bowl, or divide between individual bowls and serve.

TIP ✔ Chorizo comes in different levels of spiciness, from mild to pretty fiery, so try out some different options until you find the type you like best.

Italian sausage, fennel and kale pasta

Fennel has a wonderful mild aniseed flavour that goes well with salami, and it's good raw or braised. Don't be put off if you haven't bought it before, it's easy to prepare.

Serves 4
785 calories per serving

300g Italian-style pork and fennel sausages
1 tbsp olive oil
1 large fennel bulb (about 300g), tough outer layer removed, diced
4 garlic cloves, sliced
½ tsp dried chilli flakes
½ tsp fennel seeds
400g tin chopped tomatoes
680ml jar passata
500g wholewheat penne (rigate or plain)
100g kale, tough stems removed, chopped
Sea salt and freshly ground black pepper

To serve
1 lemon, for zesting
Freshly grated Parmesan

1 Remove the skin from the sausages. Heat the olive oil in a large sauté pan over a medium-high heat. Add the sausage meat, breaking it up with a wooden spoon. Cook for 5–10 minutes until lightly browned.

2 Add the diced fennel and cook for 5 minutes, then add the garlic, chilli flakes and fennel seeds and stir. Cook for 5 minutes, or until the fennel has softened.

3 Tip in the chopped tomatoes and passata, bring to a simmer and cook for 15–20 minutes until reduced and thickened.

4 Meanwhile, bring a large pan of salted water to the boil. Add the pasta, stir well and cook until *al dente*, about 10–12 minutes. Drain the pasta, keeping back a little of the cooking water.

5 Season the tomato, sausage and fennel sauce with salt and pepper to taste and add a splash of cooking water to loosen the sauce if needed. Stir in the kale and cook for 2 minutes, then stir in the cooked pasta.

6 Divide the pasta and sauce between warmed bowls, zest over the lemon and serve with grated Parmesan.

ONE OF THE MAIN benefits of cooking for yourself is having full control over what you eat, as you determine what goes into your meals. The recipes in this chapter give a nod to lighter eating. They are the dishes to make when you feel like something a bit less substantial – and maybe the route to go down after a big weekend!

For me, lighter cooking is all about fresh-tasting, well-balanced dishes that are satisfying but won't leave you feeling overly full. They make use of cooking methods such as grilling, griddling and quick pan-frying and they're slightly lighter on the carbs, with crunchy salads and well-dressed veg on the side. The Warm crispy salmon salad on page 99 showcases some of our fantastic summer veg, while the Tamarind chicken skewers with green mango salad on page 110 is packed with bright flavours and looks amazing. It works well on a barbecue if you have mates round at the weekend, or on a griddle over the hob for a quick midweek meal.

For something that brings a bit of a wow factor to your dinner table, the Brown butter salmon en papillote on page 105 always impresses: you unwrap the paper parcel in the middle of the table and everyone digs in. Cooking fish wrapped up like this keeps it lovely and moist without the need for lots of oil or butter, so it's a clever way to eat a bit lighter. The sausage rolls on page 114 may not sound especially healthy, but they are made with more than fifty per cent veg and lentils and have so much flavour they put pie-shop pastries to shame.

Whether you are after a quick weekend lunch, an effortless supper or looking to kick-start a new healthier eating regime, these dishes will show you that eating 'lighter' never tasted so good.

Asian-style griddled squid salad

Squid is a useful 'convenience' food, as it freezes well and cooks quickly; the freezing process even helps to tenderise it. In this fresh, crunchy salad, squid's subtle flavour and meaty texture is a lovely contrast, and a punchy dressing pulls it all together.

Serves 4
275 calories per serving

4 large squid tubes, cleaned
Vegetable oil spray, for cooking

For the dressing
3 tbsp vegetable oil
2 lemongrass stalks, white part only and tough outer layer removed, finely chopped
2 garlic cloves, finely chopped
2 tbsp fish sauce
3 tbsp sweet chilli sauce
1 tbsp light soy sauce
Juice of 1 lime

For the salad
2 shallots, thinly sliced
100g mixed baby leaves
2 handfuls of beansprouts
A handful of coriander leaves
12 cherry tomatoes, halved
4 sprigs of mint, leaves picked
1 long red chilli, finely sliced

To serve
Sweet chilli sauce, to drizzle
Lime wedges

1 Carefully slice open each squid tube so it can lie flat, and score a lattice pattern on the softer, inner surface. Cut each one into 6 equal-sized pieces and place in a bowl.

2 To make the dressing, heat the oil in a small pan, add the lemongrass and garlic and cook for 2 minutes, then remove from the heat. Add all the remaining ingredients and mix well. Leave to cool completely.

3 Add half of the dressing to the squid. Stir to coat and leave to marinate for 20 minutes.

4 For the salad, toss all the ingredients together in a bowl. Pour on the rest of the dressing, toss again and place on a large plate or divide between individual serving plates.

5 Heat a large griddle pan over a high heat. When it is smoking hot, spray with a little oil, add the squid pieces in a single layer and cook for 30 seconds on each side or until lightly charred. Depending on the size of your griddle, you may need to cook the squid in batches.

6 Place the griddled squid on top of the salad and drizzle with a little sweet chilli sauce. Serve with lime wedges for squeezing over.

Warm crispy salmon salad

This simple warm salad celebrates the best of British summer veg and it's on the table in under 30 minutes. Don't stress if you're not used to cooking fish: salmon has a higher healthy fat content than white fish so it can cope with being slightly under- or overcooked. The pan-fried crispy skin adds a fantastic extra texture to the salad.

Serves 4
670 calories per serving

1 fennel bulb, tough outer layer removed, thinly sliced
8 asparagus spears, trimmed of woody ends and finely shaved with a vegetable peeler or mandoline
8 radishes, finely sliced
4 salmon fillets, skin on, about 180g each
30g plain flour, for dusting
1 tbsp olive oil
250g tenderstem broccoli
250g fine green beans, trimmed
200ml water
1 tbsp extra-virgin olive oil
200g frozen peas
Sea salt and freshly ground black pepper

For the dressing
4 tbsp extra-virgin olive oil
1 tsp Dijon mustard
Juice of 1 lemon
2 tbsp roughly chopped dill

1 Put the fennel, asparagus and radishes into a bowl of cold water with a handful of ice added and leave to crisp up for 10 minutes or so.

2 Season each salmon fillet with salt and pepper and dust both sides with flour. Heat the olive oil in a large non-stick frying pan over a medium-high heat. Place the salmon skin side down in the pan and hold down with a spatula for 30 seconds or so. Cook, without moving, for 7–8 minutes.

3 Meanwhile, put the broccoli and beans into a sauté pan with the water and extra-virgin oil. Season well with salt and pepper. Bring to the boil and cook over a medium heat, moving the veg around so they cook evenly. When the liquid has almost all evaporated, add the frozen peas. Once the peas are cooked, remove from the heat and drain off any excess water.

4 When you can see that the skin on the fish is crispy, flip the salmon fillets over and cook for 2 minutes on the other side. Remove from the heat and leave to rest while you make the dressing.

5 Whisk the dressing ingredients together in a bowl and pour over the warm veg in the pan. Drain the fennel, asparagus and radishes and add to them the pan. Toss to mix and season with salt and pepper to taste.

6 Divide the warm salad between serving plates and top each portion with a salmon fillet, crisped skin up, to serve.

Baked sardines with carrot salad

Sardines taste amazing, so give this light fish supper a go when they're in season (roughly September to February). They are naturally quite high in healthy fats, so they stay nice and moist as they cook and provide a good contrast to the crunchy carrot salad and toasted crumb topping.

Serves 4
490 calories per serving

12 sardines, gutted and cleaned
1 tbsp extra-virgin olive oil, to drizzle
Sea salt and freshly ground black pepper

For the carrot salad
600g carrots, peeled and thinly sliced on an angle
1 tbsp sea salt
50g sultanas
50g pine nuts, toasted
2 large handfuls of flat-leaf parsley leaves
50g mixed sprouted beans and grains

For the toasted crumbs
75g sourdough bread, crusts removed, torn into pieces
1 tbsp extra-virgin olive oil
1 garlic clove, peeled and smashed

For the dressing
4 tbsp extra-virgin olive oil
3 tbsp lemon juice
1 tbsp runny honey
1 tbsp seeded mustard

To serve
Lemon wedges

1 For the salad, put the carrots into a large bowl, add the salt and mix well. Leave for 20 minutes or until the carrots have softened a little.

2 Rinse the carrots under plenty of cold running water to remove all the salt, then drain well. Clean the bowl and tip the carrots back into it. Add all the remaining salad ingredients and toss to combine.

3 Preheat the oven to 220°C/Fan 200°C/Gas 7 with the grill on. Line a baking tray with baking parchment.

4 Lay the sardines on the baking tray, drizzle with the extra-virgin olive oil and season with salt and pepper. Place on the top shelf of the oven for 8–10 minutes, until the sardines are cooked through and starting to char on the surface.

5 Meanwhile, blitz the sourdough bread in a blender to crumbs. Heat the extra-virgin olive oil with the smashed garlic clove in a frying pan over a medium heat. Add the breadcrumbs and cook, stirring, until the crumbs are evenly toasted and browned. Remove from the heat and discard the garlic clove.

6 Whisk all the dressing ingredients together in a small bowl, pour over the carrot salad and mix well.

7 Transfer the carrot salad to a serving platter or divide between individual plates and top with the sardines. Sprinkle with the toasted crumbs and serve with lemon wedges for squeezing over.

Gremolata fish with posh tartare sauce

Zesty herb- and lemon-flavoured breadcrumbs add a lovely texture to this healthier version of fish and chips. Oven-cooked potato wedges are an easy alternative to fries and they taste so much better than shop-bought frozen chips.

Serves 4
495 calories per serving

4 skinless plaice fillets, about 180g each
1 tbsp olive oil, plus a little extra for oiling
Sea salt and freshly ground black pepper

For the baked potato wedges
800g Maris Piper potatoes, cut into wedges
1 tbsp olive oil

For the gremolata crumb
100g sourdough bread, crusts removed, torn into pieces
2 tbsp parsley leaves, roughly chopped
Finely grated zest of 1 lemon

For the tartare sauce
1 large free-range egg, hard-boiled, peeled and grated
4 tbsp reduced-fat mayonnaise
4 tbsp Greek yoghurt (0% fat)
2 tbsp cornichons, finely chopped
1 tbsp baby capers, drained
2 tbsp flat-leaf parsley, finely chopped

To serve
300g green beans, steamed
Lemon wedges

1 Preheat the oven to 220°C/Fan 200°C/Gas 7. Line one large baking tray with baking parchment and lightly oil another one.

2 Place the potato wedges on the lined baking tray, drizzle with the olive oil and season with salt and pepper. Cook on the middle shelf of the oven for 30 minutes or until brown and crispy, turning the potatoes halfway through cooking.

3 Meanwhile, for the gremolata crumb, put the sourdough, parsley and lemon zest into a small food processor and pulse to fine crumbs. Tip into a bowl and set aside.

4 To make the tartare sauce, mix all the ingredients together in a bowl and season with a little salt and pepper to taste.

5 Turn the oven to the grill setting. Lay the fish fillets on the oiled baking tray. Season with salt and pepper and drizzle with the olive oil, then top each fillet with an even layer of gremolata crumb. Grill on the top shelf of the oven for 8 minutes or until the gremolata crumb is crispy and the fish is cooked. Keep a close eye on it, to make sure the topping doesn't burn!

6 Serve the fish fillets with the tartare sauce, baked potato wedges, steamed green beans and lemon wedges for squeezing over.

Brown butter salmon en papillote

This is a real event of a dish as you can bring the whole paper parcel to the table to unwrap, and then let everyone help themselves. I like to serve it as a lighter alternative to a traditional Sunday lunch. There's a little alcohol in the brown butter sauce, which will burn off during cooking.

Serves 6
550 calories per serving

800g new potatoes
80g butter
Juice of 1 lemon
**50ml anise-flavoured aperitif,
    such as Pernod**
**350g purple sprouting broccoli,
    cut into individual stems**
1kg piece of skinless salmon fillet
2 tbsp capers, drained
**Sea salt and freshly ground black
    pepper**

To serve
**A few sprigs of dill, roughly chopped
    (optional)**
Lemon wedges

1 Preheat the oven to 220°C/Fan 200°C/Gas 7.

2 Place the potatoes in a pan of boiling salted water. Bring to a simmer and cook for 10–12 minutes or until tender. Drain and leave until cool enough to handle, then slice thickly.

3 Put the butter into a small saucepan and cook over a medium heat until it turns a golden nutty brown colour. Remove from the heat and quickly add the lemon juice to stop the cooking process, then stir in the alcohol and set aside.

4 Lay a large piece of baking parchment over an oven tray (big enough to hold the salmon and more than double the width). Lay the potato slices along the middle of the paper and top with the broccoli stems.

5 Place the salmon fillet on top and season well with salt and pepper. Scatter the capers on top of the fish and spoon over the brown butter. Bring the sides of the paper up over the fish to enclose it and form a parcel. Fold the edges over to seal. Bake in the oven for 20 minutes.

6 Open the parcel and sprinkle a little chopped dill over the salmon if you like. Serve at once, with lemon wedges for squeezing over.

TIP ✔ Cooking the fish like this locks in the flavour and keeps it lovely and moist. Try it using individual salmon steaks for an easy midweek meal.

Charred trout with beetroot and orange salad

Trout is widely available, but people don't seem to buy it very often, which is a shame – they're definitely missing out! It is a lovely, light fish with a mild flavour. Here, the charring process gives it a barbecue taste, while the vibrant orange and beetroot salad provides a refreshing, sweet-sharp contrast.

Serves 4
565 calories per serving

4 trout fillets, skin on, about 180g each
Sea salt and freshly ground black pepper

For the salad
3 oranges (ideally blood/blush oranges)
6 pre-cooked medium beetroot, cut into wedges
200g watercress

For the dressing
5 tbsp extra-virgin olive oil
Juice of ½ orange (ideally blood/ blush orange)
Juice of 1 lemon
3 tbsp sherry vinegar
1½ tsp Dijon mustard

To finish
50g hazelnuts, toasted and roughly chopped

1 Preheat the oven to 220°C/Fan 200°C/Gas 7. Line a baking tray with baking parchment.

2 For the salad, peel the oranges, removing all the white pith, then slice them thickly and place in a bowl. Add the beetroot and watercress.

3 Place the trout skin side up on the lined baking tray and season with salt and pepper. Cook in the oven for 4 minutes. Take the fish from the oven and gently peel off the skin, then wave a cook's blowtorch all over the fish until it is starting to char in places.

4 For the dressing, whisk the ingredients together and season with salt and pepper to taste.

5 Pour half of the dressing over the salad and toss well then divide between 4 plates. Top with the trout and scatter over the toasted hazelnuts. Drizzle with the remaining dressing to serve.

TIP ✔ Blood oranges, which are sometimes labelled as 'blush oranges', have a relatively short season – from January to March. If you can't find them, use regular oranges instead.

Spicy beef lettuce cups

Lettuce leaves are used to scoop up the beef stir-fry for this tasty light dinner. They also provide a welcome fresh crunch and balance the fiery Asian flavours.

Serves 4
415 calories per serving

500g lean beef mince (5% fat)
1 tbsp vegetable oil
1 onion, finely sliced
2 garlic cloves, finely chopped
2.5cm piece of fresh ginger, finely grated
1 red chilli, finely sliced
150g carrot, peeled and julienned
150g kohlrabi, peeled and julienned
100g green beans, cut into 2.5cm lengths
75g water chestnuts, sliced
100g beansprouts
150g cooked vermicelli, roughly chopped
2 tbsp Shaoxing rice wine
2 tbsp Sriracha hot sauce
1 tbsp soy sauce
2 tbsp kecap manis (sweet soy sauce)

To serve
3 Little Gem lettuces, leaves separated
4 spring onions, finely sliced on an angle
40g roasted cashew nuts, roughly chopped
Lime wedges

1 Preheat the oven to 200°C/Fan 180°C/Gas 6. Line a large baking tray with baking parchment.

2 Spread the beef mince out on the lined baking tray and cook in the oven for 40 minutes, breaking it up well with a wooden spoon every 10 minutes. It should have a dark, even colour and resemble large coffee granules. Remove from the oven; set aside.

3 Place a wok over a high heat and add the oil. When it begins to smoke, add the onion, garlic and ginger and stir-fry for 1 minute.

4 Next add the chilli, carrot, kohlrabi and green beans and stir-fry for another 3–4 minutes.

5 Add the water chestnuts, beansprouts, vermicelli, cooked beef mince, rice wine and all the sauces. Stir-fry for another 2 minutes, adding 1–2 tbsp water if it gets a little dry.

6 Divide the stir-fry between warmed bowls and place on large plates, with the lettuce leaves alongside. Scatter with spring onions and chopped cashews and serve with lime wedges for squeezing over.

Tamarind chicken skewers with green mango salad

Tamarind paste adds a sweet-and-sour tang to these simple chicken skewers (it's sold in jars and available from most larger supermarkets). You will also need six long wooden skewers – soak them before using, so they don't burn on the griddle.

Serves 6
415 calories per serving

750g skinless, boneless chicken thighs
5 tbsp tamarind paste
3 tbsp soy sauce
3 tbsp fish sauce
Juice of 1 lime
5 tbsp brown sugar
4cm piece of fresh ginger, finely grated

For the green mango salad
750g firm green (unripe) mangoes, peeled
1 shallot, thinly sliced
1-2 long red chillies, thinly sliced
1½ tsp light brown sugar
Juice of 1½ limes
1½ tbsp fish sauce
A large handful of coriander leaves, roughly chopped

To serve
Lime wedges

1 Cut each chicken thigh into quarters. Place in a bowl along with the tamarind, soy sauce, fish sauce, lime juice, brown sugar and ginger. Mix well and leave to marinate for at least 20 minutes. Meanwhile, soak the wooden skewers in a tray of warm water.

2 For the salad, cut the mango flesh away from the stone, then slice it into julienne strips and place in a large bowl. Add all the remaining ingredients and toss together to combine.

3 Drain the skewers and thread the marinated chicken chunks on to them. Heat a large griddle over a medium heat. Cook the skewers on the griddle for about 5 minutes on each side, until charred and cooked through.

4 Pile the chicken skewers onto a large warmed plate and serve with lime wedges for squeezing over and the green mango salad alongside.

Chicken and coleslaw tray bake

Sweet roasted cabbage works so well with the chicken and veg in this easy oven bake. The crispy roast chicken skin is crumbled on top to add an extra layer of seasoning. For a lighter lunch, you could halve the chicken amount and serve one escalope each.

Serves 4
470 calories per serving

4 boneless chicken breasts, skin on
1 small white cabbage, cut into
**   8 wedges**
2 tbsp extra-virgin olive oil
300ml chicken stock
2 red onions, thinly sliced
2 carrots, peeled and julienned
2 fennel bulbs, tough outer layer
**   removed, thinly sliced**
1 tbsp fennel seeds, toasted and
**   crushed**
Sea salt and freshly ground black
**   pepper**

For the dressing
3 tbsp reduced-fat mayonnaise
1 tbsp Dijon mustard
1 tbsp white wine vinegar
2 tbsp flat-leaf parsley, finely
**   chopped**

To serve
1 lemon, for zesting

1 Preheat the oven to 220°C/Fan 200°C/Gas 7. Line a baking sheet with baking parchment.

2 Remove the skins from the chicken breasts, scrape them clean with a sharp knife and lay on the lined baking sheet. Cover with a second layer of parchment and place another baking sheet on top.

3 Place the cabbage wedges in a lined roasting tray and drizzle with half the olive oil. Cook on the top shelf of the oven, with the tray of chicken skins on the middle shelf, for 12–15 minutes. Take the chicken skins out of the oven and leave to cool between the trays.

4 Pour the chicken stock over the cabbage, add the red onions, carrots and fennel, and season with salt and pepper. Return the tray to the oven for 20 minutes.

5 Meanwhile, slice the chicken breasts horizontally in half to make 8 large, thin escalopes. Season both sides with salt, pepper and fennel seeds. Drizzle with the remaining 1 tbsp olive oil. Preheat the grill to high.

6 Remove the tray of veg from the oven and place the chicken escalopes on top. Place under the grill for 5–7 minutes until the chicken is just cooked.

7 For the dressing, whisk the ingredients together in a bowl, adding 1 tbsp of the juices from the roasting tray if it is too thick.

8 Divide the chicken and veg between warmed plates and trickle over the dressing. Crumble the chicken skin and zest the lemon over each plate to serve.

Pork, lentil and veg sausage rolls

Who doesn't love a sausage roll?! The filling in these is more than fifty per cent veg, making them much healthier than most shop-bought options. They are a great alternative to a pie, and are also delicious eaten cold, so pack into lunchboxes to take to work, or on a picnic. ❄

LIGHTER DISHES

Makes 8
550 calories per sausage roll

500g block of ready-made puff pastry
Plain flour, for dusting
1 free-range egg, beaten, for brushing
2 tbsp sesame seeds

For the filling
1 tbsp olive oil
1 onion, finely chopped
150g courgette, grated
150g carrot, peeled and grated
2 garlic cloves, grated
2 tsp fennel seeds, toasted and lightly crushed
450g sausage meat
400g tin brown lentils, drained
2 tbsp sage leaves, finely chopped
Sea salt and freshly ground black pepper

1   To make the filling, heat the olive oil in a large frying pan over a high heat, then add the onion and cook for 5 minutes, or until softened.

2   Squeeze the courgette in your hands to remove all excess liquid, then add to the pan with the carrot, garlic and fennel seeds. Cook for a further 5 minutes, stirring often. Tip into a large bowl and leave to cool.

3   When the veg mixture is cooled, add the sausage meat, lentils, chopped sage and some salt and pepper. Mix well, then divide in half.

4   Roll out the puff pastry on a lightly floured surface to a large rectangle, about 40 x 25cm. Cut in half, so each piece measures 25 x 20cm. Have the shorter side of each piece facing you.

5   Shape one half of the sausage filling into a log down the right-hand side of one piece of pastry, leaving a 1cm clear margin along the surrounding three edges. Brush the right edge and the top and bottom edges with a little egg wash. Fold the pastry from the left-hand side over the filling to enclose it and press the edges together to seal, using a fork.

6   Repeat with the other piece of pastry and the rest of the filling. Place both filled pastry rolls in the fridge for an hour to rest and firm up.

7   Preheat the oven to 200°C/Fan 180°C/Gas 6. Line a baking tray with baking parchment.

8 Take the pastry rolls out of the fridge, cut each one into 4 even lengths, and place on the lined tray. Brush with beaten egg and sprinkle with sesame seeds. Bake for 30–35 minutes or until golden brown.

9 Leave the sausage rolls on the baking tray for a few minutes to cool slightly, then serve with a mixed leaf salad on the side.

To freeze: Before you cook the sausage rolls, wrap them well and freeze. Defrost in the fridge and then cook as above.

Broccoli and quinoa salad

Quinoa doesn't taste of much, but it readily takes on other flavours and is a good alternative to rice or couscous. You can eat this fresh green salad hot or cold, so it's ideal to make in advance or pack into a lunchbox. It also makes a great side dish. ⋁

Serves 4
435 calories per serving

150g mixed quinoa (red, white and
    black), rinsed
1 tsp Swiss vegetable bouillon
    powder
550ml water
1 tsp light olive oil
250g broccoli, cut into small florets
250g asparagus spears, trimmed
    and cut into 2.5cm lengths
150g frozen edamame beans
150g frozen peas
A handful of mint leaves, roughly
    chopped
A handful of flat-leaf parsley leaves,
    roughly chopped
Sea salt and freshly ground black
    pepper

For the dressing
Juice of 1 lemon
1 tsp Dijon mustard
5 tbsp extra-virgin olive oil

To serve
2 Little Gem lettuces, roughly
    chopped
70g rocket leaves
200g feta cheese
1 ripe avocado, quartered, stoned
    and sliced

1 Put the quinoa and bouillon powder into a small saucepan and pour on 450ml of the cold water. Stir well and place over a medium-high heat. When it comes to the boil, lower the heat and simmer for 15 minutes, or until all the liquid has been absorbed. Tip the quinoa onto a tray and spread out to cool.

2 Heat the olive oil in a large sauté pan over a high heat. Add the broccoli and cook for 3–4 minutes, then add the asparagus with the remaining 100ml water and cook for 2–3 minutes.

3 Add the edamame beans and peas, stir well and season with salt and pepper. Cook until the beans and peas have defrosted, then remove from the heat. Drain off any excess water from the pan then tip the contents of the pan onto another tray to cool.

4 For the dressing, whisk the lemon juice, mustard and extra-virgin olive oil together in a small bowl until combined. Season with salt and pepper and set aside.

5 Once the quinoa and cooked veg are cooled, put them into a large bowl with the chopped herbs and toss to combine.

6 Place the lettuce and rocket in the bottom of a serving bowl and fill with the broccoli and quinoa salad. Crumble over the feta and add the avocado slices. Drizzle with the dressing to serve.

Russian roasted veg salad

Roasting the vegetables adds an extra layer of flavour to this spin on the famous salad, which is also lighter and healthier than the classic version, because it's made with much less mayonnaise. It's a wonderful way to showcase the diversity of taste, texture and colour in root veg. ♡

Serves 4
305 calories per serving

300g carrots, peeled
300g potatoes, peeled
300g swede, peeled
300g turnips, peeled
300g beetroot, peeled
2 tbsp extra-virgin olive oil
1 tbsp caraway seeds
200g frozen peas
4 Little Gem lettuces
**Sea salt and freshly ground black
pepper**

For the dressing
4 tbsp reduced-fat mayonnaise
3 tbsp Greek yoghurt (0% fat)
1 shallot, finely diced
**30g cornichons, finely sliced, plus
1 tbsp pickle juice from the jar**
1 tsp Dijon mustard
**2 tbsp flat-leaf parsley, finely
chopped**

1 Preheat the oven to 220°C/Fan 200°C/Gas 7. Line two large baking trays with baking parchment.

2 Cut the carrots, potatoes, swede and turnips into 2cm chunks; cut the beetroot into 1.5cm chunks. Place all the root veg on the lined baking trays and drizzle with olive oil, then sprinkle with salt, pepper and the caraway seeds. Cook on the top two oven shelves for 45 minutes, giving the veg a stir halfway through.

3 Meanwhile, for the dressing, mix the ingredients together in a bowl until combined. If the dressing is too thick, add a little water to loosen it.

4 Add the frozen peas to a small pan of boiling water, bring back to a simmer and blanch for 1 minute, then drain in a sieve and refresh under cold running water; set aside. Separate the lettuce leaves and cut each one in half lengthways.

5 Remove the tray of roasted veg from the oven and leave to cool.

6 To serve, divide the lettuce between serving plates and top with the roasted veg. Scatter the peas over the salad and spoon on the dressing.

Roasted Moroccan carrots with lentils

North African spices are more subtle and aromatic than fiery and hot, so in this dish they bring out the natural sweetness of the carrots. This warm salad is great on its own as a light lunch or dinner, but it will also work well as a side with some simply cooked chicken or fish. ♡

Serves 4
495 calories per serving

800g baby carrots (assorted colours, ideally), scrubbed
1 tbsp cumin seeds, lightly crushed
1 tbsp Aleppo pepper flakes
3 tbsp blossom honey
3 tbsp extra-virgin olive oil
1 onion, finely chopped
3 celery sticks, finely diced
3 garlic cloves, sliced
1 tbsp ras el hanout
2 x 250g packs cooked Puy lentils
2 tbsp water
A handful each of parsley and mint, roughly chopped
150g feta cheese, crumbled
Sea salt and freshly ground black pepper
1 lemon, to serve

1 Preheat the oven to 220°C/Fan 200°C/Gas 7. Line two baking trays with baking parchment.

2 If any of the baby carrots are bigger than the others, cut them so that they are all an even size, then place all the carrots on the lined baking trays.

3 Sprinkle the carrots with the crushed cumin and pepper flakes and drizzle with the honey and 2 tbsp of the extra-virgin olive oil, sharing equally between the trays. Season with salt and pepper. Roast in the oven for 20–25 minutes, giving the carrots a good stir halfway through cooking.

4 Meanwhile, heat the remaining 1 tbsp oil in a sauté pan. Add the onion and cook for 4–5 minutes until it starts to turn brown. Add the celery and garlic and cook for another 2 minutes.

5 Stir in the ras el hanout and cook for 1 minute, then add the cooked lentils with the water and warm through. Remove from the heat and stir in half the chopped herbs.

6 Divide the lentils between warmed bowls and pile the roasted carrots on top. Scatter over the remaining herbs and crumbled feta, then zest over the lemon. Cut the lemon into wedges and serve on the side.

THERE ARE SO MANY amazing vegetables on supermarket shelves these days that the idea of every meal revolving around meat seems limiting and quite old-fashioned. Cutting down on meat and including more vegetables in your diet is not only a step forward for your health and the planet, it's going to be a positive influence on your bank balance too. If you replace even just a few of your usual meat-based meals with veggie ones, you'll quickly notice how much you save.

If, up until now, veg shopping has tended to centre on the standard trio of potatoes, carrots and onions, this is your chance to try something new and exciting. Beetroot lends the risotto on page 135 an amazingly vibrant colour, while butternut squash gives the pasta bake on page 154 a luxurious creamy sauce. There are eight varieties of veg and beans in the Minestrone on page 132, so each mouthful provides a different texture and taste. And do give the curry on page 156 a go – I guarantee even the most passionate of sprout haters will be converted!

Vegetables are so versatile, it's high time we celebrated them properly, promoting them to be the central hero of a meal more often, rather than just sitting on the side. From pizzas and curries to pasta dishes, tray bakes and even filo-wrapped veg parcels (page 128), I hope the recipes in this chapter will encourage you to cook more veg-centred meals. You'll be impressed by their fantastic depth of flavour, I promise.

Roasted vegetables and rocket pesto

Using rocket to make pesto is a nice alternative to the usual basil, adding an extra peppery flavour and taking it to another level. Any leftover pesto can be stirred through pasta – it keeps well in the fridge in a jar topped with a layer of olive oil. ♡

VEGGIE SUPPERS

Serves 4
700 calories per serving

**400g long beetroot (or round
   beetroot, cut into wedges)**
400g rainbow carrots
300g baby parsnips
400g butternut squash
2 tbsp extra-virgin olive oil
1 tbsp fennel seeds
2 baby cauliflowers, halved
**500g hispi cabbage, cut into
   4 wedges**
**Sea salt and freshly ground black
   pepper**

For the rocket pesto
90g rocket leaves
1 garlic clove, grated
25g pine nuts, toasted
25g basil leaves
40g Parmesan, finely grated
Juice of ½ lemon
120ml extra-virgin olive oil
2 tbsp light olive oil

To finish
25g pine nuts, toasted
A handful of rocket leaves

1 Preheat the oven to 220°C/Fan 200°C/Gas 7. Line two roasting trays with baking parchment.

2 Peel the beetroot, carrots and parsnips, and cut away the skin from the butternut squash. You want the veg to be in similar-sized pieces to ensure they cook evenly, so cut any larger root veg in half lengthways and then cut the squash into similar-sized wedges. Place in a single layer in the roasting trays. Drizzle with the extra-virgin olive oil and sprinkle with salt, pepper and the fennel seeds. Roast for 20 minutes.

3 Take the trays out, add the cauliflower and cabbage and turn to coat in the oil. Swap the oven shelf position of the trays and cook for a further 20 minutes.

4 Meanwhile, make the rocket pesto. Have a large bowl filled with water and ice to hand. Bring a pan of water to the boil, add a pinch of salt, then plunge the rocket into the pan and blanch very briefly. As soon as it's wilted, scoop it out with tongs or a slotted spoon and drop it into the iced water to cool quickly.

5 Drain the rocket and squeeze out all water. Place in a small food processor and add the garlic, pine nuts, basil, Parmesan, lemon juice and both olive oils. Blend until smooth. Season with salt and pepper to taste.

6 Once the vegetables are cooked, share them between warmed plates and drizzle with the rocket pesto. Scatter over the toasted pine nuts and fresh rocket leaves. Serve straight away.

Feta and greens filo triangles

For these parcels, filo pastry provides a crunchy contrast to the creamy feta and leafy green filling, which is also balanced by a sweet and sharp tomato chilli sauce. ♡

VEGGIE SUPPERS

Makes 6
385 calories per serving

Olive oil spray
1 onion, finely chopped
4 garlic cloves, finely chopped
250g cavolo nero, trimmed of thick stems and chopped
250g spinach, chopped
250g chard, chopped (including stems)
250g reduced-fat feta cheese, crumbled
50g pine nuts, toasted
A bunch of dill (20g), roughly chopped
½ nutmeg, freshly grated
Finely grated zest of 1 lemon
6 sheets of filo pastry, each 45 x 25cm
Sea salt and freshly ground black pepper
Sesame seeds, to sprinkle

For the tomato chilli sauce
50g caster sugar
50ml red wine vinegar
400g tin chopped tomatoes
½ tsp dried chilli flakes

1 Heat 10 sprays of olive oil in a large frying pan over a high heat. Add the onion and sauté for 4–5 minutes until softened, adding a splash of water if it starts to stick. Add the garlic and cook for another 2 minutes. Add the cavolo nero and cook for 2–3 minutes to soften slightly. Stir through the spinach and chard, then take off the heat; the spinach will have wilted only a little. Season with salt and pepper. Leave to cool completely.

2 Meanwhile, for the sauce, put the sugar in a small saucepan over a medium-high heat and swirl gently until melted and starting to turn to a caramel. Take off the heat and immediately add the vinegar, stirring to make a syrup. Add the tomatoes, chilli flakes and a pinch of salt. Simmer for 20 minutes until thickened.

3 Preheat the oven to 220°C/Fan 200°C/Gas 7. Mix the feta, pine nuts, dill, nutmeg and lemon zest into the cold greens. Divide into 6 portions. Unroll the filo; keep under a damp tea towel to stop the sheets drying out.

4 Lay a sheet of filo on your work surface with a short edge facing you and brush the edges with a little oil. Place a portion of filling at the lower end, about 1.5cm from the bottom and left hand edges and form into a triangular shape. Fold over the right half of the pastry sheet, then fold the bottom left filo corner over the filling to make a triangle. Fold the parcel up to form another triangle. Keep folding over and up until you reach the top. Seal the edge with a little oil. Spray with a little oil, sprinkle with sesame seeds and place on a baking tray. Bake for 20–25 minutes until golden and crispy. Serve with the warm tomato chilli sauce.

Miso ramen

So many amazing Japanese flavours are breaking through into the foods we eat now, and this one-bowl meal shows them off a treat. It's a good one to try if you're not sure about the taste of tofu, as it is fried in a delicious sweet and sticky glaze. ∨

Serves 4
355 calories per serving

5 tbsp miso paste
1.5 litres water
2 tbsp soy sauce
2.5cm piece of fresh ginger, grated
12 shiitake mushrooms
225g smoked tofu, cut into 4 slices
2 tbsp liquid aminos
250g soba noodles
16 baby corn
1 tbsp vegetable oil
8 baby pak choi
200g beansprouts
2 red chillies, finely sliced on an angle
2 spring onions, finely sliced on an angle
4 tbsp crispy seaweed
2 tbsp black sesame seeds
1 tbsp sesame oil, to finish

1 Place the miso, water, soy sauce, ginger and shiitake in a large saucepan. Stir to mix in the miso, then bring to a very gentle simmer. Let simmer for 5 minutes.

2 Meanwhile, place the smoked tofu in a shallow bowl and pour on the liquid aminos. Turn the tofu slices over to make sure they are soaked well on both sides.

3 Bring a pan of salted water to the boil. Add the soba noodles, bring back to the boil and cook until just tender, about 5 minutes.

4 Add the baby corn to the miso broth and cook for a further 4 minutes.

5 Meanwhile, heat the oil in a non-stick frying pan over a high heat. Lift the tofu out of its bowl, shaking off any excess liquid aminos; save this. Gently place the tofu in the frying pan and cook for 2–3 minutes on each side until browned. Now add the reserved liquid aminos to the pan (it will bubble up) and let it reduce to a glaze. Remove from the heat.

6 As soon as the soba noodles are cooked, drain them in a colander and rinse under cold water, then divide between 4 serving bowls. Add the pak choi to the miso broth and remove from the heat.

7 Divide the pak choi, baby corn and beansprouts between the bowls. Ladle over the miso broth and add the tofu. Garnish with red chillies, spring onions and crispy seaweed. Sprinkle with sesame seeds, drizzle over the sesame oil and serve straight away.

Minestrone

It takes a bit of effort to get all the veg prepped and ready for this minestrone, but it's totally worth it as you'll be rewarded with a hearty soup that is packed with layer upon layer of flavour and texture. Keep portions stashed in the freezer for a quick midweek evening meal, or to take to work in a flask for a nourishing lunch. ♡ ❄

Serves 8
420 calories per serving

4 tbsp olive oil
2 onions, diced
3 carrots, peeled and diced
2 small sweet potatoes, peeled and diced
3 leeks, well washed, halved lengthways and chopped
4 celery sticks
8 garlic cloves, sliced
2 x 400g tins chopped tomatoes
2 litres vegetable stock
4 sprigs of rosemary, leaves picked, finely chopped
1 tsp dried Italian mixed herbs
200g dried wholemeal spiral pasta
200g green beans, trimmed and cut into 3cm lengths
100g greens (cavolo nero, cabbage, spinach)
400g tin borlotti beans, drained
2 handfuls of basil leaves, finely chopped
4 tbsp sun-dried tomato pesto
Sea salt and freshly ground black pepper

To finish
1 large courgette, grated
50g Parmesan, finely grated

1   Heat the olive oil in a large pan over a medium-high heat. Add the onions, carrots and sweet potatoes and cook, stirring occasionally, for 15–20 minutes or until softened and caramelised. Add the leeks, celery and garlic and cook for a further 5 minutes.

2   Tip in the tinned tomatoes, pour in the vegetable stock and add the chopped rosemary and dried herbs. Bring to a simmer and allow to simmer gently for 10 minutes.

3   Meanwhile, break the pasta spirals in half. Add the pasta to the pan and cook for a further 8 minutes.

4   Now add the green beans, greens and borlotti beans and cook for a further 5 minutes. Stir in the chopped basil and sun-dried tomato pesto and season with salt and pepper to taste.

5   Ladle the minestrone into warmed bowls, scatter over the grated courgette and then grate over lots of Parmesan to serve.

To freeze minestrone: Cool and pack into one- or two-portion tubs (without any courgette or Parmesan on top) then freeze. Defrost fully in the fridge overnight. Reheat in a pan over a medium heat (or microwave on high) until hot right through. Finish with grated courgette and Parmesan.

Beetroot risotto with goat's cheese

This special risotto makes the most of a classic flavour pairing and it has an amazing colour. The walnuts break up the smooth texture of the rice and goat's cheese, while the seaweed flakes act as a salty, umami seasoning. ♥

Serves 4
755 calories per serving

500g pre-cooked beetroot, peeled
1.25 litres vegetable stock
1 tbsp butter
1 tbsp olive oil
3 long shallots, finely chopped
2 garlic cloves, finely chopped
300g risotto rice
250ml red wine
1 tbsp chopped thyme leaves
50g Parmesan, finely grated
Sea salt and freshly ground black
pepper

For the dressing
80g butter
1 tbsp red wine vinegar
1 tbsp chopped thyme leaves
75g walnuts, toasted and roughly
broken

To finish
100g goat's cheese log, cut into
8 slices
2 tsp dulse/kombu seaweed flakes
2 handfuls of rocket leaves

1 Put 300g of the cooked beetroot into a small food processor and blitz until smooth. Pour the vegetable stock into a saucepan, add the beetroot purée and heat gently. Roughly chop the remaining beetroot; set aside.

2 Melt ½ tbsp butter in a large saucepan over a medium heat. Add the olive oil, then the shallots and cook for about 5 minutes until just softened. Add the garlic and cook for 1 minute. Add the rice, stir to coat, then cook for 3–4 minutes to lightly toast it.

3 Pour in the wine, add the thyme and cook, stirring, until most of the liquid has been absorbed. Now add the beetroot stock, a ladleful at a time, stirring constantly and allowing the liquid to be absorbed before adding the next ladleful. Continue for about 20 minutes, until the rice is cooked but still slightly *al dente* and all the liquid has been absorbed. Taste for seasoning, adding salt and pepper as needed.

4 Meanwhile, for the dressing, melt the 80g butter in a small pan until it turns a golden brown. Take off the heat and add the wine vinegar to stop the cooking. Add the thyme, walnuts and chopped beetroot.

5 Preheat the grill to high. When the risotto is ready, remove from the heat and stir though the remaining butter and the Parmesan. Lay the goat's cheese on a baking tray and grill for 2–3 minutes until browned.

6 Divide the risotto between warmed bowls and top with the dressed beetroot. Add the goat's cheese slices and sprinkle with seaweed flakes. Finish with the rocket.

Pumpkin and spinach dhal

The lentils and pumpkin absorb the other flavours exceptionally well in this creamy curry. The pumpkin also adds a delicious sweetness, which is counterbalanced by the ginger and spices, making it a lovely, warming meal. You can use butternut squash if you can't find pumpkin. ♡ ❄

Serves 4
420 calories per serving
735 calories with raita and paratha

2 tbsp vegetable oil
1 onion, sliced
3 garlic cloves, chopped
2.5cm piece of fresh ginger, grated
1 tbsp black mustard seeds
1 tbsp cumin seeds
1 tsp ground turmeric
A handful of curry leaves
600g wedge of peeled pumpkin, cut into 2cm dice
400g red lentils
1.2 litres vegetable stock
2 dried red chillies
400ml full-fat coconut milk
150g baby spinach
Sea salt and freshly ground black pepper

To finish and serve
Coriander leaves
Parathas, ready-made (optional)
Raita (page 172, optional)

1 Heat the oil in large non-stick saucepan over a high heat. Add the onion and cook for 5–8 minutes, until golden brown.

2 Add the garlic and ginger, cook for 2–3 minutes, then add the mustard and cumin seeds and cook for 1 minute until fragrant.

3 Add the turmeric, curry leaves and diced pumpkin, stir well and cook for 5 minutes. The mixture will be quite dry, so keep stirring regularly so it doesn't catch on the bottom of the pan.

4 Add the lentils, vegetable stock and dried chillies and bring to a simmer. Cook, stirring a few times, for 15 minutes or until the lentils become tender and the pumpkin is cooked.

5 Stir in the coconut milk and simmer for 5 minutes. Add the spinach and stir until it wilts.

6 Serve scattered with coriander, with parathas and raita alongside if you wish.

To freeze: Allow to cool, then pack in one- or two-portion containers and freeze. Defrost fully in the fridge, then reheat in a saucepan over a medium-low heat until hot all the way through.

Curried vegetable patties

Full flavoured, with a lovely chunky texture, these patties are really satisfying. The naans are so simple and tasty, you'll want to make some every time you prepare a curry. ♡

Serves 6
565 calories per serving

500g potatoes, peeled
500g carrots, peeled
500g parsnips, peeled
3 tbsp vegetable oil
2 tbsp medium Madras curry powder
1 onion, finely chopped
1 tsp cumin seeds
2 garlic cloves, finely chopped
200g Savoy cabbage, shredded
200g frozen peas
400g tin chickpeas, drained
**Sea salt and freshly ground black
    pepper**

For the naan
**250g self-raising flour, plus extra
    for dusting**
250g natural yoghurt (0% fat)
1 tsp sea salt
Vegetable oil, for brushing
1 tbsp nigella seeds

For the mango and lime mayo
2 tbsp natural yoghurt (0% fat)
1 tbsp reduced-fat mayonnaise
1 tbsp mango chutney
1 tbsp lime pickle, finely chopped

To serve
Salad leaves
Sliced cucumber

1 Preheat the oven to 200°C/Fan 180°C/Gas 6. Line a large roasting dish with baking parchment.

2 Cut the root veg into 2cm chunks, and place in the roasting dish. Drizzle with 1 tbsp oil, sprinkle with salt, pepper and the curry powder and toss well. Roast for 40–50 minutes until tender, turning halfway through.

3 Meanwhile, to make the naan dough, mix the flour, yoghurt and salt together in a large bowl. Remove from the bowl and knead the dough until smooth, then wrap in cling film and set aside.

4 When the veg are ready, take them out of the oven (leave it on) and let cool slightly. Heat 1 tbsp oil in a non-stick frying pan over a medium-high heat and add the onion with the cumin seeds. Sauté for 3–4 minutes to soften, then add the garlic and cook for 2–3 minutes. Toss in the cabbage and cook for 5–6 minutes, until tender. Remove from the heat and stir in the peas.

5 Put the chickpeas into a food processor and pulse to mash lightly. Add the roasted veg and pulse again to mix; the mixture will be quite stiff. Scrape into a large bowl, stir through the cabbage mix and season with salt and pepper. With wet hands, form into 6 patties.

6 You'll need to cook the patties in batches. Heat the remaining 1 tbsp oil in a large non-stick frying pan. Add 2 or 3 patties and cook for 3–4 minutes on each side or until slightly crispy. Transfer to a baking tray. Repeat to cook the rest. Place the tray in the oven for 10 minutes to finish cooking. Meanwhile, for the mango and lime mayo, mix all the ingredients together in a bowl.

7 Divide the naan dough into 6 pieces. Roll out on a lightly floured surface to a tear-drop shape, 5mm thick. Heat a griddle pan over a high heat. Cook the naan in batches: brush one side with oil and lay on the griddle, oiled side down. Brush the top with oil and sprinkle with a few nigella seeds. Cook for 1–2 minutes on each side until browned and lightly puffed. Remove and wrap in a tea towel to keep warm. Repeat to cook the rest.

8 Place a naan on each warmed plate and top with a veg patty. Serve the salad and mayo on the side.

Romanesco, corn and coconut curry

Romanesco is like a cross between broccoli and cauliflower, and it has an amazing, subtle flavour. If you can't find it, use ordinary cauliflower, as it's closer in texture than broccoli and holds its shape better in this curry. This is a great midweek recipe, as it mainly uses store-cupboard ingredients. ∨

Serves 4
465 calories per serving
715 calories with rice

2 tbsp vegetable oil
2 tsp cumin seeds
1 onion, finely chopped
4 garlic cloves, finely chopped
2 tsp ground coriander
1 tsp ground turmeric
1 tsp garam masala
500g romanesco cauliflower,
    cut into florets
300ml vegetable stock
400ml coconut milk
350g tin sweetcorn, drained
200g frozen peas
A handful of coriander, chopped
Sea salt and freshly ground black
    pepper

For the fried paneer
225g paneer, cut into cubes
½ tsp ground turmeric
½ tsp sea salt
1 tbsp vegetable oil

To serve
1 long red chilli, finely sliced
300g basmati and wild rice, cooked
    (optional)

1 Heat the oil in a large non-stick pan over a high heat. Add the cumin seeds, let them sizzle for a few seconds then add the onion. Cook for 5 minutes, then add the garlic and cook for another 2 minutes.

2 Lower the heat, add the ground spices and stir for 1 minute, then add the romanesco florets and stir-fry for 1 minute. Pour in the vegetable stock and half the coconut milk and cook for 20 minutes.

3 Meanwhile, prepare the paneer. Put it into a bowl with the turmeric and salt and mix well. Heat the oil in a non-stick frying pan over a medium-high heat. Add the paneer and cook until browned well on all sides, about 5–8 minutes. Remove from the heat.

4 Add the remaining coconut milk to the romanesco pan and stir though the sweetcorn, peas, fried paneer and half the coriander. Bring to a simmer and cook gently for another 5 minutes. Taste to check the seasoning, adding salt and pepper as needed.

5 Serve the curry scattered with the sliced red chilli and remaining coriander and accompanied by the rice, if serving.

Portobello mushroom tray bake

For this easy tray bake, portobello mushrooms are piled high with a delicious lentil filling then topped with blue cheese and grilled. Choose a medium strength cheese, such as Stilton; Roquefort is likely to be too strong and will overpower the dish. ♡

VEGGIE SUPPERS

Serves 4
640 calories per serving

1 small onion
1 carrot, peeled
**2 celery sticks, de-stringed with
    a veg peeler**
4 thick slices of sourdough bread
2 tbsp olive oil
**4 large portobello mushrooms,
    stems removed**
4 garlic cloves, finely sliced
2 x 250g packs cooked Puy lentils
150ml vegetable stock
1 tbsp thyme leaves
100g blue cheese
**Sea salt and freshly ground black
    pepper**

For the salad
**180g mixed rocket, watercress and
    spinach**
Juice of ½ lemon, or to taste
1 tbsp extra-virgin olive oil

1 Preheat the oven to 200°C/Fan 180°C/Gas 6. Line a baking tray with baking parchment.

2 Using a food processor, pulse the onion, carrot and celery until finely chopped.

3 Lay the slices of sourdough on the lined baking tray and drizzle with half the olive oil. Place a mushroom, cup side up, on each slice of sourdough.

4 Heat the remaining olive oil in a large non-stick sauté pan over a medium heat. Add the onion, carrot, celery and garlic and cook for 10–15 minutes or until softened and starting to caramelise.

5 Add the lentils, vegetable stock and thyme leaves and cook for 5 minutes, or until the liquid is reduced by half. Remove from the heat and season with salt and pepper to taste.

6 Spoon the lentil mix into the mushroom cavities, piling it up high. Bake in the oven for 20 minutes, then remove and turn on the grill.

7 Crumble the blue cheese on top of the filled mushrooms and place under the grill for 5 minutes, or until the cheese has melted.

8 Meanwhile, in a bowl, dress the salad leaves with a little lemon juice, extra-virgin olive oil, salt and pepper. Serve the mushrooms straight away, with the leafy salad on the side.

Penne with roasted red pepper sauce

This may look like a very basic pasta dish but the sauce has so much complexity and depth – created by slow-cooking the onion with the tomato purée and blowtorching the roasted peppers before blending everything to a rich, smooth sauce. ♡ ❄

Serves 4
585 calories per serving

2 tbsp olive oil
1 onion, finely chopped
3 tbsp tomato purée
400g whole roasted peppers from a jar (drained weight)
4 garlic cloves, sliced
½ tsp sweet smoked paprika
300ml whipping cream
A handful of basil leaves (10g)
500g dried penne pasta
Sea salt and freshly ground black pepper
Freshly grated Parmesan, to serve

1 Heat the olive oil in a non-stick sauté pan over a medium-high heat. Add the onion and cook for 5 minutes, until starting to soften. Add the tomato purée, stir well and cook over a medium-low heat for 8–10 minutes, stirring occasionally.

2 Meanwhile, slit the peppers open down one side and lay them flat on a baking tray. Pat dry with kitchen paper, then wave a cook's blowtorch over them until they are blackened and blistered in parts. Set aside.

3 Add the garlic and smoked paprika to the sauté pan and cook for 2–3 minutes. Add the roasted peppers and cream and simmer for 5 minutes. Stir in half of the basil and season with salt and pepper. Remove from the heat, tip into a blender and blitz until smooth.

4 Bring a pan of salted water to the boil. Add the pasta and cook until *al dente*, about 10–12 minutes.

5 While the pasta is cooking, return the blended sauce to the sauté pan and bring to a gentle simmer. Taste to check the seasoning and adjust as necessary.

6 Once the pasta is cooked, drain in a colander, saving some of the water. Add the pasta to the sauce, with a splash of the water, and toss to mix. If the sauce is too thick, add a little more pasta water. Serve in warmed bowls, sprinkled with Parmesan and the remaining basil.

To freeze the sauce: Let cool, then freeze portions in tubs. Defrost in the fridge and reheat in a small pan over a medium-low heat until hot right through.

New potato, spinach and goat's cheese frittata

I'm a big fan of baked omelettes. They are quick and easy, and good for using up any leftovers you might have lurking in the fridge. They also work well either hot or cold, so take a slice to work for a healthy alternative to your usual sandwich lunch. ▽

Serves 4
445 calories per serving

2 tbsp olive oil
400g new potatoes, diced
1 large red onion, finely diced
8 large free-range eggs
100ml single cream
½ tsp freshly grated nutmeg
A handful of mint leaves, finely chopped
3 garlic cloves, sliced
150g spinach, chopped
120g goat's cheese, roughly chopped
12 sage leaves
Sea salt and freshly ground black pepper

1 Preheat the oven to 220°C/Fan 200°C/Gas 7. Heat the olive oil in a large ovenproof frying pan over a medium-low heat. Add the diced potatoes with a pinch of salt and cook for 8–10 minutes. Toss in the red onion and cook for a further 5 minutes.

2 Meanwhile, crack the eggs into a large bowl. Add the cream, nutmeg, chopped mint and some salt and pepper and whisk well; set aside.

3 Add the garlic to the pan and cook for 2 minutes, then toss in the spinach and sauté until it begins to wilt. Pour the cream mixture into the pan, stir around for 1 minute, then remove from the heat.

4 Dot the goat's cheese evenly over the surface of the frittata and scatter over the sage leaves. Place on the top shelf of the oven for 8–10 minutes until the egg has set and the cheese is golden.

5 Remove the frittata from the oven and leave to stand for a few minutes to cool slightly before serving.

TIP ✔ This veggie frittata uses a classic combination of flavours, but feel free to vary the ingredients using whatever is in your fridge – diced cooked peppers, onions, peas or mushrooms, crumbled feta or sliced spring onions, for example.

Veggie bolognaise

Soya protein mince is a good meat-free alternative for a traditional bolognaise and this is such an intensely flavoured sauce that you won't feel like you're missing out on the meat. The slowly caramelised vegetables create a rich base for the sauce and getting in all that flavour early on gives the sauce an incredible taste. ♡ ❄

Serves 6–8
375–500 calories per serving

1 onion, roughly chopped
2 large carrots, peeled and roughly
    chopped
4 celery sticks, roughly chopped
4 garlic cloves, peeled
2 tbsp olive oil
4 tbsp tomato purée
250ml red wine
680g jar passata
400g tin chopped tomatoes
3 tbsp Swiss vegetable bouillon
    powder
½ tsp dried chilli flakes
750ml water
2 red peppers, finely chopped
200g baby chestnut mushrooms,
    quartered
1 tbsp dried oregano
4 sprigs of rosemary, leaves picked,
    finely chopped
750g dried spaghetti
100g soya protein mince
Sea salt and freshly ground black
    pepper
Freshly grated Parmesan, to serve

1 Put the onion, carrots, celery and garlic into a food processor and pulse a few times to chop finely. Heat the olive oil in a large non-stick saucepan over a high heat. Add the chopped veg and cook for 20 minutes or until softened and starting to caramelise, stirring often. Lower the heat to medium.

2 Stir in the tomato purée and cook for a further 5–8 minutes, stirring to ensure it doesn't catch or burn. Pour in the wine and simmer until reduced by half. Add the passata, chopped tomatoes, bouillon powder and chilli flakes, then pour in the water and bring to a simmer. Add the peppers, mushrooms and herbs and cook gently for 20 minutes.

3 Meanwhile, bring a large pan of salted water to the boil. Add the spaghetti and cook until *al dente*.

4 Stir the soya mince through the sauce and cook for a further 2–3 minutes, until nicely thickened. Season with salt and pepper to taste.

5 Drain the spaghetti and divide between warmed bowls. Spoon on the sauce and grind over some pepper. Serve with lots of Parmesan grated over.

To freeze the sauce: Allow to cool then freeze in a sealed container. Defrost fully in the fridge, then reheat in a saucepan over a medium heat until hot right through.

Easy homemade pizzas

This is a fun way to get the whole family involved in mealtimes. Everyone can roll out their own pizza dough base and then pile on their favourite toppings. Just lay out a range of topping ingredients to choose from (if you want to include some meat options, then that's totally up to you). Everyone's happy! Just don't add too many toppings or the base won't get nice and crispy. ♡ ❄

Serves 4
710 calories per serving (plus chosen toppings)

For the pizza dough
400g strong white bread flour (or '00' flour)
100g semolina flour, plus extra for dusting
½ tsp fine sea salt
325ml tepid water
7g sachet fast-action dried yeast
1 tsp caster sugar
2 tbsp extra-virgin olive oil

For the tomato sauce
680ml jar passata
3 garlic cloves, grated
2 tsp dried oregano
Sea salt and freshly ground black pepper

For the cheese layer
320g reduced-fat mozzarella (80g per pizza), grated

1 To make the pizza dough, sift the flours into a large bowl, mix in the salt and make a well in the centre. Measure the warm (but not hot) water into a jug. Stir in the yeast, sugar and extra-virgin oil and set aside to activate for 5 minutes.

2 Pour the yeast liquid into the flour well and mix until the dough starts to come together. Transfer to a lightly floured surface and knead to a smooth dough. To knead, use the heel of one hand to stretch the dough away from you, then fold it back over itself and turn the dough 90°. Repeat and continue until you have a nice smooth ball of dough; this will take around 10 minutes.

3 Place the dough in a large bowl dusted lightly with semolina flour, cover the bowl with a damp cloth and leave in a warm place until the dough has doubled in size, about 45 minutes – 1 hour.

4 Meanwhile, to make the tomato sauce, pour the passata into a saucepan and add the garlic, oregano and some salt and pepper. Bring to a simmer over a medium heat and simmer gently for 10 minutes. Taste and adjust the seasoning if necessary, then remove from the heat and set aside to cool down.

5 Preheat the oven to 250°C/Fan 240°C/Gas 10. Place two baking trays (preferably without a lip) inside to heat up.

Toppings
Choose a selection from:

New potatoes, thinly sliced
Herbs (sage, basil, oregano)
Courgette, thinly sliced
Red onion, finely sliced
Mushrooms, thinly sliced
Chargrilled artichokes, quartered
Pitted green or black olives
Red or green chilli, sliced
Roasted peppers, cut into strips
Parmesan, finely grated
Rocket leaves (top the pizza with these just before serving)

6 Turn out the pizza dough onto a clean surface, knock back (or knead again to knock out the air) and divide into 4 equal portions. Shape each into a ball. Roll out one ball of dough on a lightly floured surface to a thin round.

7 Sprinkle a baking sheet (not preheated) with a little semolina flour and lift the pizza base onto it. Spoon 3–4 tbsp tomato sauce into the middle and spread it out over the dough, leaving a 1–2cm clear margin around the edge. Scatter 80g grated mozzarella over evenly, then add your choice of pizza toppings, distributing them evenly over the sauce.

8 When you are ready to cook, gently shake the pizza tray to loosen the base from it. Open the oven door, pull a heated tray out halfway and slide the pizza onto the hot tray, closing the oven door as soon as possible to keep the heat in. Bake for 8–12 minutes or until the cheese has melted and the dough is golden brown.

9 Repeat to shape, assemble and bake the remaining pizzas. Either serve each pizza straight away, as it comes out of the oven, or keep warm in a second low oven until they are all ready.

To freeze leftover tomato sauce: Allow to cool, then freeze in a sealed container. Defrost fully in the fridge before using.

Illustrated overleaf

Creamy butternut squash pasta bake

Rich and creamy, this could easily become a new favourite at home. It's also a great way of getting a big portion of veg into your family without them even noticing! It's all about the toppings: crunchy seeds and breadcrumbs, sweet chunks of butternut squash and nuggets of acidity from the sun-blushed tomatoes. ♡ ❄

Serves 6
575 calories per serving

1kg butternut squash, cut into chunks (about 2cm)
1 tbsp olive oil
500g macaroni
Sea salt and freshly ground black pepper

For the cheese sauce
60g butter
60g plain flour
1 litre whole milk
1 tbsp liquid aminos
60g Parmesan, finely grated
¼ tsp freshly grated nutmeg

For the topping
A handful of sage leaves
40g sun-blushed tomatoes, roughly chopped
50g fresh breadcrumbs
2 tbsp pumpkin oil (or use olive oil)
2 tbsp pumpkin seeds

1 Preheat the oven to 220°C/Fan 200°C/Gas 7. Line a large roasting tray with baking parchment.

2 Place the squash in the roasting tray. Drizzle with the olive oil, season with salt and pepper and toss to coat. Cook on the top shelf of the oven for 25 minutes or until the squash is tender and browned at the edges. Remove from the oven and let cool slightly for a couple of minutes. (Keep the oven on.)

3 Tip three-quarters of the roasted squash into a blender and blitz to a purée; set the rest aside.

4 Bring a large pan of salted water to the boil. Add the macaroni and cook until almost *al dente* (2–3 minutes less than the time suggested on the packet).

5 Meanwhile, for the sauce, melt the butter in a large saucepan over a medium heat. Add the flour and cook, stirring, for 1 minute, then whisk in the milk and cook, whisking, until the sauce thickens slightly. Lower the heat and add the liquid aminos, Parmesan and nutmeg. Stir until the cheese has melted, then stir through the squash purée to make a rich, smooth sauce. Take off the heat and season with salt and pepper to taste.

6 Drain the macaroni, add to the sauce and stir well. Tip into a large, deep baking dish, about 25 x 30cm. Scatter over the rest of the roasted squash, the sage, sun-blushed tomatoes and breadcrumbs. Drizzle with the oil. Place on the middle shelf of the oven, turning on the oven grill at the same time. Bake for 10 minutes.

7 Take out the dish, scatter the pumpkin seeds evenly over the surface and return to the oven for 5 minutes or until the topping is golden. Serve at once, with a green salad.

To freeze: Cool and pack in a lidded foil tray (or several trays). Defrost fully in the fridge, then remove the lid and reheat in an oven preheated to 200°C/Fan 180°C/Gas 6 for 30 minutes, until hot all the way through. If the surface appears to be browning too quickly, cover loosely with foil.

Roasted winter sprout curry

This is a fantastic way of getting people to eat Brussels sprouts, even if they claim not to like them. It's such a full-flavoured dish that it also works well as a side on Christmas day with roast turkey. As a midweek winter meal, serve the curry with rice and parathas or flatbreads, or the naans on page 138. ⋁

page 138

Serves 4
660 calories per serving
975 calories with raita and paratha

800g Brussels sprouts, halved
1 tbsp caraway seeds
1 tbsp cumin seeds
1 tbsp ground turmeric
2 tbsp ground coriander
3 tbsp vegetable oil
2 onions, thinly sliced
4 garlic cloves, sliced
2 long green chillies, thinly sliced
    and deseeded
500ml vegetable stock
100g desiccated coconut, toasted
A handful of coriander, finely
    chopped
50g flaked almonds, toasted
Sea salt and freshly ground black
    pepper

For the paneer
1 tsp vegetable oil
225g paneer, cut into cubes
½ tsp ground turmeric

To serve
Parathas, ready-made (optional)
Raita (page 172, optional)

1   In a large bowl, toss the sprouts with the whole and ground spices and season with salt and pepper.

2   Heat half the oil in a large saucepan over a high heat, add the onions and cook for 5–10 minutes or until they are starting to brown. Add the remaining oil with the garlic and chillies and cook for 1 minute.

3   Toss in the sprouts and stir-fry for 2–3 minutes. Pour in the vegetable stock, bring to a gentle simmer and cook for 10–15 minutes, stirring a few times.

4   Meanwhile, to cook the paneer, heat the 1 tsp oil in a non-stick frying pan over a medium-high heat. Add the paneer, sprinkle with the turmeric and a pinch of salt and toss the pan to coat the paneer in the seasoning. Cook for 4–5 minutes, tossing the pan regularly, until the cubes are browned all over.

5   When the sprouts are tender, stir through the paneer and coconut. Taste and adjust the seasoning if necessary, then toss through the chopped coriander and toasted almonds. Serve at once, with parathas and raita if you like.

WE ALL LIVE BUSY LIVES and it can be easy to resort to convenience food. But, from first-hand experience, I also know that all those takeaways, quick-cook ready meals and high-calorie snacks are only going to make things worse in the long run.

When life gets hectic, we rely on food to give us the energy we need to power on through, so it should be properly nutritious. If lack of time is one of the reasons you're struggling to cook from scratch every day, spend a morning or afternoon every now and then cooking to create meals for your freezer. You may want to eat part of the food you've cooked straight away then freeze the rest, or you might want to portion up the whole lot into freezable containers. Either way, you'll be creating your own freezer meals, ready to take out, defrost and reheat when needed – proper, homemade convenience food!

For this chapter I've created plenty of recipes that are perfect for batch cooking, such as tasty curries, meatballs, fish cakes and a cheesy lasagne. And some of these dishes taste even better after they have been frozen because the flavours have had longer to mellow and become friends. Butternut squash and chickpea curry (page 167) is a really good example of this.

Of course, I'm not totally against all convenience food. But I guarantee that if you make a little effort up front, you will reap the benefits. You'll feel more in control of the food you and your family eat, you'll be eating better-quality and healthier meals – and you'll be saving money too. Investing a little time now means you're much less likely to give in to any junk food temptations when you're tired and hungry.

Moroccan chicken with preserved lemons

Preserved lemons are such a wonderful ingredient. Chopped up, they create the fantastic bitter-sweet, summery layer of flavour running through this dish, which complements the heady north African spices. Keep a jar of them in the fridge to bring life to tagines and stews, couscous and rice dishes, salads and dressings. ❄

Serves 6
565 calories per serving

1 tbsp olive oil
12 skinless, bone-in chicken thighs
3 onions, cut into 2.5cm wedges
6 garlic cloves, sliced
1 tsp ground ginger
½ tsp ground cinnamon
1 tbsp ras el hanout
4 carrots, peeled and cut into
    2.5cm pieces
600g potatoes, peeled and cut
    into 2.5cm pieces
1 litre chicken stock
A large pinch of saffron strands
120g green olives, drained
4 preserved lemons (from a jar),
    chopped
Sea salt and freshly ground black
    pepper

For the couscous
1 tsp olive oil
400g wholewheat giant couscous
600ml chicken stock

To finish
A handful of coriander leaves,
    roughly chopped

1 Heat the olive oil in large non-stick sauté pan over a high heat. Season the chicken well on both sides with salt and pepper. Lay 6 chicken thighs in the pan and cook, turning until golden brown on both sides, then remove to a plate. Repeat with the remaining thighs.

2 Add the onions to the pan and cook over a medium heat for 5 minutes to soften. Add the garlic and cook for 1 minute. Sprinkle in the ground ginger, cinnamon and ras el hanout and stir for 30 seconds. Add the carrots, potatoes, chicken stock and saffron. Bring to the boil, lower the heat and simmer for 10 minutes.

3 Return the chicken to the pan and add the olives and preserved lemons. Put a lid on the pan and simmer gently for 15–20 minutes or until the veg are tender.

4 Meanwhile, for the couscous, heat the olive oil in a saucepan over a medium heat. Tip in the couscous and toast gently, stirring occasionally, for 2–3 minutes until golden. Pour in the chicken stock and cook gently until the couscous is tender and the liquid has evaporated. Season well with salt and pepper.

5 Serve the Moroccan chicken in warmed bowls with the couscous, scattered with chopped coriander.

To freeze: Cool and freeze the chicken (but not the couscous) in two-portion lidded foil trays. Defrost fully in the fridge overnight. Cover loosely with foil, and reheat in an oven preheated to 200°C/Fan 180°C/Gas 6 for 30 minutes or until piping hot.

BATCH COOKING

Chicken and pearl barley soup

When it's chilly outside, make a big batch of this warming soup for a comforting supper, or take it to work in a flask for an easy lunch. Dried mushrooms lend lots of flavour here. They are a great store-cupboard ingredient to have on hand for pepping up soups, pasta sauces, stews and casseroles. ❄

Serves 6
670 calories per serving
690 calories with Parmesan

4 tbsp olive oil
1 onion, diced
3 large carrots, peeled and diced
3 garlic cloves, peeled and sliced
4 celery sticks, diced
2 courgettes, diced
2 leeks, trimmed, well washed
    and diced
2 litres fresh chicken stock
1 litre water
A bunch of thyme sprigs, tied
    with string
2 bay leaves
250g pearl barley
40g dried porcini mushrooms
1.5kg free-range whole chicken,
    spatchcocked or quartered,
    skin removed
200g cavolo nero, tough stalks
    removed, chopped roughly
250g frozen peas
Sea salt and freshly ground black
    pepper
Extra-virgin olive oil, to drizzle
30g Parmesan, freshly grated,
    to serve (optional)

1 Heat the olive oil in a large flameproof casserole dish over a medium-high heat. Add the onion and carrots and cook, stirring often, for 5 minutes. Add the garlic, celery, courgettes and leeks and cook for a further 5 minutes, or until softened.

2 Pour in the chicken stock and water and add the thyme, bay leaves, pearl barley and dried porcini. Stir and bring to a gentle simmer.

3 Lay the chicken in the casserole, season generously with pepper and simmer gently for 1 hour, turning the chicken over halfway through cooking.

4 Lift the chicken out of the broth onto a plate and allow to cool a little. Remove and discard the thyme and bay leaves from the broth. When the chicken is cool enough to handle, remove the meat from the bone and shred into bite-sized pieces.

5 Bring the broth back to a simmer and stir in the cavolo nero and peas. Cook for 2 minutes, then return the chicken to the soup and stir well. Taste to check the seasoning and add salt and pepper if needed.

6 Ladle into warmed bowls and drizzle with extra-virgin olive oil. Best served with grated Parmesan.

To freeze: Allow to cool, then freeze in two-portion containers. Defrost fully in the fridge overnight, then reheat in a saucepan over a medium heat, until hot all the way through.

Chicken and new potato curry

If you haven't made a curry before, this is a great recipe to start off with, as it is based on ingredients and flavours that everyone knows and understands instinctively. ❄

Serves 6
535 calories per serving
690 calories with rice, poppadoms
   and salad

2 tbsp vegetable oil
2 large onions, finely diced
**7cm piece of fresh ginger, finely
   grated**
6 large garlic cloves, finely grated
A large handful of curry leaves
2 tsp ground coriander
2 tsp ground cumin
2 tsp paprika
2 tsp ground turmeric
2 tsp garam masala
1 tsp hot chilli powder
6 whole cloves
6 cardamom pods, crushed
2 cinnamon sticks
2 tsp salt
400ml carton passata
**1.5kg skinless, boneless chicken
   thighs, halved**
200ml chicken stock
600g Jersey Royal potatoes, halved
**A handful of coriander leaves,
   chopped, to finish**

To serve (optional)
Cooked brown basmati rice
**Poppadoms (cooked in the
   microwave)**
**Cucumber, tomato and red
   onion salad**

1 Heat the oil in a large saucepan over a high heat. Add the onions and cook for 10 minutes or until softened and well browned.

2 Add the ginger, garlic and curry leaves and cook for 2–3 minutes. Lower the heat and add the ground and whole spices and salt. Cook, stirring, for 1 minute.

3 Pour in the passata, bring to a simmer and cook over a low heat, stirring often, for 2 minutes to create an aromatic base.

4 Add the chicken thighs and stock, stir well and bring back to a gentle simmer. Put the lid on and cook for 10 minutes.

5 Stir in the potatoes, then cover and simmer gently for 30 minutes, stirring every 10 minutes or so to make sure the curry doesn't catch on the bottom on the pan. Remove the lid and cook for a further 10–15 minutes until the liquor has reduced slightly.

6 Serve scattered with chopped coriander, with brown rice and poppadoms if you like. A refreshing cucumber salad is lovely on the side.

To freeze: Allow the curry to cool, then freeze in two-portion containers. Defrost fully in the fridge overnight, then reheat in a saucepan over a medium heat until hot all the way through. You may need to add a little extra liquid to loosen the curry as you reheat it.

Illustrated overleaf

BATCH COOKING

Butternut squash and chickpea curry

Butternut squash and chickpeas are a great combination and, if you mostly stick to staples like carrots and potatoes, this curry is a nice way of trying out different veg. This is also a good example of a dish that actually tastes better when it is reheated, as the flavours mellow and develop over time. ♡ ❄

Serves 6
425 calories per serving
590 calories with rice and salad

3 tbsp vegetable oil
2 tbsp black mustard seeds
1 tbsp cumin seeds
12 cardamom pods, split
A handful of curry leaves
2 large onions, finely chopped
5 garlic cloves, grated
5cm piece of fresh ginger, finely grated
2 tsp ground turmeric
1 tsp ground cumin
2 tbsp ground coriander
1 litre hot vegetable stock
1kg peeled, deseeded butternut squash (prepared weight), cut into 2.5cm chunks
250ml coconut cream
2 x 400g tins chickpeas, drained
200g green beans, cut into 2.5cm lengths

To serve (optional)
3 x 250g pouches ready-cooked pilau rice
Cucumber, tomato and red onion salad

1 Heat the oil in a large non-stick saucepan over a high heat, then add the mustard and cumin seeds, cardamom pods and curry leaves. Cook, stirring, for 30 seconds, or until the mustard seeds begin to pop.

2 Add the onions to the pan and cook, stirring often, for 8 minutes or until softened and starting to brown.

3 Toss the garlic and ginger into the pan and cook for 2 minutes. Lower the heat a little, stir in the ground spices and cook, stirring, for 1 minute.

4 Pour in the vegetable stock and bring to the boil. Add the butternut squash, bring back to the boil, then lower the heat and simmer for 15 minutes.

5 Stir in the coconut cream, chickpeas and beans and cook for 10–15 minutes or until the liquor is reduced and thickened slightly. Meanwhile, heat up the pouches of rice mix, following the packet instructions, if using.

6 Serve the curry in warmed bowls, with hot pilau rice and a cucumber salad on the side if you like.

To freeze: Let the curry cool, then freeze in two-portion containers. Defrost fully in the fridge overnight, then reheat in a saucepan over a medium heat until hot all the way through. You may need to add a little extra liquid to loosen the curry as you reheat it.

Illustrated overleaf

Italian turkey meatballs

These healthy meatballs include grated carrots and courgettes to help keep them moist as they cook. Baking – rather than frying – them at a high heat brings down the fat content and caramelises the outside a little, to delicious effect. ❄

Serves 8
350 calories per serving
450 calories with bread and salad

2 tbsp light olive oil
1 onion, finely chopped
2 carrots, peeled, finely grated and squeezed to remove excess liquid (about 275g prepared weight)
2 courgettes, finely grated and squeezed to remove excess liquid (about 500g prepared weight)
1kg turkey mince (mixed breast and thigh meat)
4 tbsp finely chopped sage
2 tbsp dried Italian herbs
75g fresh breadcrumbs
100g Parmesan, finely grated
4 garlic cloves, finely chopped
2 tbsp tomato purée
2 x 400g tins chopped tomatoes
680g jar passata
1 tsp caster sugar
2 tsp fennel seeds, toasted and finely ground
500ml water
2 handfuls of basil leaves, finely chopped
Sea salt and freshly ground black pepper

To serve
Flat-leaf parsley, finely chopped
Crusty bread (optional)
Leafy side salad (optional)

1 Heat 1 tbsp olive oil in a large, deep saucepan over a medium heat. Add the onion and cook, stirring often, for 7–10 minutes until softened. Remove with a slotted spoon to a plate and leave to cool.

2 Preheat the oven to 250°C/Fan 240°C/Gas 10. Line two large baking trays with baking parchment.

3 In a large bowl, combine the cooled onion, grated carrots and courgettes, turkey mince, sage, dried herbs, breadcrumbs and half the Parmesan. Season with salt and pepper and mix well. Form into 48 even-sized balls. Place on the baking trays and bake for 10–15 minutes until browned all over, turning once halfway through.

4 Meanwhile, heat the remaining olive oil in the large saucepan. Add the garlic and cook for 2 minutes. Stir in the tomato purée and cook, stirring, for 2 minutes, then add the tinned tomatoes, passata, sugar, fennel seeds and water. Bring the sauce to a gentle simmer and cook gently for 20 minutes.

5 Add the baked meatballs to the sauce and cook for 10 minutes, then stir in the chopped basil.

6 Serve in warmed shallow bowls, sprinkled with the rest of the Parmesan and the chopped parsley. Serve with crusty bread and a green side salad, if you like.

To freeze: Allow to cool, then freeze in two-portion lidded foil trays. Defrost fully in the fridge overnight. Reheat in a saucepan over a medium heat until the meatballs are hot all the way through.

Beef biriyani

Cooking the mince in the oven first intensifies its flavour for this delicious curry. It's a complete meal in one that freezes brilliantly – great to have on standby in the freezer for occasions when life gets so busy you have little time to cook. ✳

Serves 8
440 calories per serving
480 calories with raita

1kg beef mince (10% fat)
2 tbsp vegetable oil
2 onions, diced
2 carrots, peeled and diced
4 garlic cloves, finely chopped
5cm piece of fresh ginger, finely grated
200g Madras curry paste
1 tsp hot chilli powder (optional)
500g basmati rice
1.5 litres beef stock
200g courgettes, diced
200g green beans, cut into 2.5cm lengths
200g cauliflower, cut into very small florets
200g broccoli, cut into very small florets
200g frozen peas
A handful of coriander leaves, roughly chopped

For the raita (optional)
400g Greek strained yoghurt (0% fat)
1 tsp cumin seeds, toasted and ground
1 cucumber, grated
A little chopped mint
Sea salt

1 Preheat the oven to 200°C/Fan 180°C/Gas 6. Line a large baking tray with baking parchment.

2 Spread the beef out on the lined baking tray and cook in the oven for 40 minutes, breaking up the mince well with a wooden spoon every 10 minutes. It should have a dark, even colour and resemble large coffee granules. Remove from the oven and set aside.

3 Heat the oil in a large saucepan over a high heat. Add the onions and cook, stirring often, for 5 minutes to soften. Toss in the carrots and cook for 3–4 minutes.

4 Add the garlic and ginger and cook for 2–3 minutes. Stir in the curry paste and chilli powder, if using, and cook, stirring, for 1–2 minutes.

5 Add the basmati rice to the pan and cook, stirring, for 2 minutes. Pour in the beef stock, bring to the boil and boil rapidly for 5–8 minutes, stirring occasionally, until most of the liquid has evaporated and the rice is just slightly undercooked. Lower the heat to a simmer.

6 Add the roasted mince, along with any juices, to the pan. Add the courgettes, green beans, cauliflower and broccoli and stir well. Put a lid on the pan and simmer for 8–10 minutes, until the rice and veg are cooked and the liquid is all absorbed.

7 To make the raita, if serving, put the yoghurt into a bowl and add the cumin and a pinch of salt. Squeeze the cucumber to remove all excess liquid and add to the bowl. Mix well and sprinkle with chopped mint.

8 Stir the frozen peas through the biriyani and cook for a couple of minutes, or until the peas are tender. Scatter the chopped coriander over the biriyani. Serve straight away, in warmed bowls, with the raita alongside if serving.

To freeze: Allow to cool, then freeze in two-portion lidded foil trays. Defrost fully in the fridge overnight. Add a splash of water and cover loosely with foil, then reheat in an oven preheated to 200°C/Fan 180°C/ Gas 6 for 30 minutes or until hot right through.

Beef and stout stew

There's nothing quite like a comforting beef stew on a cold wintry day. Made with classic ingredients, this is a traditional stew with big, bold flavours. The alcohol will cook off in the oven, but stout has quite a powerful taste so if you're cooking for kids you may prefer to replace it with extra beef stock. ❄

Serves 6
515 calories per serving
740 calories with mash

3 tbsp vegetable oil
**1.5kg braising beef, cut into
    3.5cm pieces**
4 large onions, thickly sliced
3 tbsp plain flour
500ml stout
800ml beef stock
6 sprigs of thyme
450g chestnut mushrooms, halved
**A handful of flat-leaf parsley, finely
    chopped**
**Sea salt and freshly ground black
    pepper**
**Mashed potatoes (see page 208),
    to serve (optional)**

1 Preheat the oven to 170°C/Fan 150°C/Gas 3.

2 Place a large non-stick casserole pan over a high heat and add 1 tbsp oil. Season the beef with salt and pepper and brown in the hot casserole in batches until the pieces are well coloured on both sides, making sure you do not overcrowd the pan. Remove each batch and set aside on a plate.

3 Add the remaining oil to the pan and lower the heat to medium. Toss in the onions and cook for about 10 minutes until softened and golden brown. Stir in the flour and cook, stirring, for 1–2 minutes.

4 Add the stout and stir well to deglaze the pan, scraping up the meat sediment. Return the beef to the pan, pour in the beef stock and add the thyme. Bring to the boil, then put the lid on the casserole and cook in the oven for 1½ hours.

5 Add the mushrooms to the casserole, stir well and return to the oven for a further 1½ hours.

6 Season with salt and pepper to taste and stir in half of the chopped parsley. Scatter over the remaining parsley to finish and serve with mash, if you like.

To freeze: Allow to cool, then freeze in two-portion lidded foil trays. Defrost fully in the fridge overnight. Cover with foil, then reheat in an oven preheated to 200°C/Fan 180°C/Gas 6 for 30 minutes, or until hot right through.

Sausage and bean casserole

Butterbeans and sausages are a fantastic pairing and this casserole brings in some really gorgeous ingredients. Choose good-quality sausages – traditional or flavoured if you prefer. Lincolnshire or Cumberland sausages are a good place to start. It is quite a loose sauce, so serve with lots of crusty bread to soak it all up. ❄

BATCH COOKING

Serves 6
735 calories per serving
835 calories with bread

12 large pork sausages
1 tbsp olive oil
4 cooking chorizo sausages,
    thickly sliced
2 red onions, diced
4 garlic cloves, sliced
2 red peppers, cored, deseeded
    and cut into 2.5cm pieces
2 yellow peppers, cored, deseeded
    and cut into 2.5cm pieces
2 tsp hot smoked paprika
1 tsp ground cumin
2 tbsp thyme leaves
250ml red wine
2 x 400g tins chopped tomatoes
500ml chicken stock
2 x 400g tins butterbeans
1 tbsp sherry vinegar
2 handfuls of flat-leaf parsley,
    roughly chopped
Sea salt and freshly ground black
    pepper
Crusty bread, to serve (optional)

1 Preheat the oven to 200°C/Fan 180°C/Gas 6. Line a baking tray with baking parchment.

2 Lay the pork sausages on the lined baking tray and cook in the oven for about 15 minutes, or until browned but not fully cooked all the way through.

3 Meanwhile, heat the olive oil in a large, deep frying pan over a medium heat, add the sliced chorizo and cook for 5 minutes, until browned and crispy. Remove from the pan and set aside.

4 Add the diced red onions to the pan and cook for 7–10 minutes until softened. Add the garlic and peppers and cook for a further 5 minutes. Stir in the ground spices, then add the thyme and wine. Allow to bubble until the liquor has reduced by half, about 5–7 minutes.

5 Add the tinned tomatoes, chicken stock, browned sausages and chorizo. Cook for 20 minutes, then stir in the butterbeans and sherry vinegar and cook for a further 5 minutes. Stir through half the parsley.

6 Serve scattered with the remaining chopped parsley and with plenty of crusty bread alongside for soaking up the tasty juices, if you like.

To freeze: Allow to cool, then freeze in two-portion containers. Defrost fully in the fridge overnight, then reheat in a saucepan over a medium-low heat, stirring occasionally, until hot all the way through.

Salt cod and saffron fish cakes

Infused with saffron and flecked with peas and roasted peppers, these fish cakes are delicious. All they need is a dollop of aïoli, a squeeze of lemon and a side salad. ❄

Makes 6
415 calories per serving
550 calories with aïoli

600g cod fillet, skin removed
4–5 large baking potatoes (1.5kg)
300ml vegetable stock
2 tbsp olive oil
1 red onion, finely diced
200g roasted red peppers (from a jar), drained and diced
100g frozen peas
Finely grated zest of 1 lemon
3 tbsp plain flour, for dusting
Sea salt and freshly ground black pepper

For the salt and saffron cure
80g sea salt
30g caster sugar
A large pinch of saffron strands
1 tbsp aniseed-flavoured aperitif, such as Pernod
1 tbsp olive oil
2 tbsp white wine

For the parsley salad
4 handfuls of flat-leaf parsley leaves
1 red onion, finely sliced
60g caper berries
2 tbsp extra-virgin olive oil
Juice of ½ lemon

To serve
Aïoli, good-quality, shop-bought (optional)
Lemon wedges

1 For the cure, mix all the ingredients together in a bowl. Check the cod for any pin-bones, then cut into two equal pieces and place in a container in which they fit snugly. Spread the cure all over the fish and place in the fridge for 3 hours.

2 Preheat the oven to 200°C/Fan 180°C/Gas 6. Prick the potatoes all over with a fork, place on a baking tray and bake in the oven for about 1½ hours until tender. Remove and leave until cool enough to handle. Turn the oven down to 160°C/Fan 140°C/Gas 3.

3 Take the fish from the container and rinse well under cold running water for 5 minutes to remove the cure. Place in a small roasting tin and pour over the stock. Cover with foil and bake for 20 minutes. Remove and leave the fish to cool completely in the stock.

4 Meanwhile, heat ½ tbsp of the olive oil in a frying pan over a medium heat. Add the onion and cook for 5–7 minutes until softened. Add the roasted peppers and peas and cook for about 3 minutes until the peas are tender. Remove the pan from the heat.

5 Cut the cooled potatoes in half, scoop out the flesh from the skins into a bowl and mash lightly. Drain the fish and flake into the bowl. Add the onion and pepper mix, with the lemon zest and salt and pepper to taste. Divide into 6 portions and shape into patties. Place on a tray in the fridge to chill and firm up for 1 hour.

6 Line a large baking tray with baking parchment. Heat the remaining 1½ tbsp olive oil in a large non-stick frying pan. Dust the fish cakes with flour and fry, in

batches, over a medium-high heat for 3–4 minutes on each side, until golden and crisp. Transfer to the baking tray. Once all the fish cakes have been fried, cook them in the oven for 15 minutes, until hot right through.

7 For the salad, toss all the ingredients together in a bowl and season with salt and pepper. Serve the fish cakes with the salad, aïoli and lemon wedges.

To freeze: Freeze the floured fish cakes on a baking tray, then transfer to a freezer container. Defrost fully in the fridge overnight, then cook as per the recipe.

Veggie shepherd's pie

My mum always added curry powder to her shepherd's pie and I've used it here in this delicious veggie version. It brings out the flavours of the other ingredients without overpowering them. The colourful swede and sweet potato topping adds extra flavour but you could use plain mashed potato if you prefer. ♡ ❄

Serves 10
455 calories per serving

2 tbsp olive oil
2 onions, diced
4 carrots, peeled and diced
4 garlic cloves, finely chopped
5cm piece of fresh ginger, finely grated
3 tbsp medium Madras curry powder
2 x 250g packs cooked Puy lentils
2 tbsp Swiss vegetable bouillon powder
2 x 400g tins chopped tomatoes
2 x 400g tins brown lentils, drained
700ml water
1 large head of broccoli, cut into florets
300g frozen peas
2 tbsp butter, melted

For the swede and sweet potato mash topping
1.2kg swede, peeled and diced into small cubes
1.2kg sweet potatoes, peeled and diced into small cubes
4 tbsp butter
150ml whole milk
125ml single cream
Sea salt and freshly ground black pepper

1 First prepare the mash. Put the swede into a large pan of salted water and bring to the boil. Cook for 15 minutes, then add the sweet potato and cook for a further 15 minutes or until both veg are tender. Drain in a colander, then return to the pan and mash until smooth. Add the butter, milk and cream, mix well and season with salt and pepper to taste. Set aside.

2 While the veg are cooking, preheat the oven to 220°C/Fan 200°C/Gas 7. Heat the oil in a large pan over a high heat. Add the onions and cook, stirring often, for 5 minutes to soften. Toss in the carrots and cook for 5 minutes. Add the garlic and ginger and cook for 2–3 minutes. Sprinkle in the curry powder and stir for 1 minute, then add the bouillon powder, tinned tomatoes, lentils and water. Bring to a simmer and cook for 15–20 minutes or until reduced slightly.

3 Meanwhile, blitz the broccoli in a food processor until finely chopped. Add to the lentil mixture along with the peas, and stir to combine. Transfer to a large roasting tray, about 38 x 27cm and 8cm deep.

4 Spoon the mash on top and brush with butter. Bake for 20 minutes, then turn the grill on to high and cook for a further 5–7 minutes until golden brown on top.

To freeze: Allow to cool, then freeze in two-portion lidded foil trays. Defrost fully in the fridge overnight. Cover loosely with foil and reheat in an oven preheated to 200°C/Fan 180°C/Gas 6 for 30 minutes, or until hot.

Seven vegetable lasagne

With the classic flavours and robustness of a traditional lasagne but without the meat, this will convince anyone that home-cooked food wins out over ready meals. ♡ ❄

Serves 10
650 calories per serving

3 aubergines, sliced into 1cm rounds
800g butternut squash, peeled and
    cut into 5mm slices
2 tbsp finely chopped rosemary
3 tbsp extra-virgin olive oil
4 portobello mushrooms, thickly
    sliced
500g dried wholemeal lasagne
2 large courgettes, thinly sliced
    on an angle
400g roasted red peppers (from
    a jar), drained and torn into
    thick strips
400g chargrilled artichokes (from
    a jar or tub), drained and halved
150g cavolo nero, stalks removed,
    roughly chopped
Sea salt and freshly ground black
    pepper

For the tomato sauce
1 tbsp olive oil
1 large onion, finely chopped
4 garlic cloves, finely chopped
2 tsp dried oregano
400g tin chopped tomatoes
2 x 680g jars passata
450ml water

For the cheese sauce
100g butter
100g wholemeal flour
1.25 litres skimmed milk
¼ tsp freshly grated nutmeg
100g reduced-fat strong Cheddar,
    grated
50g Parmesan, finely grated
3 x 125g balls reduced-fat mozzarella

1 Preheat the oven to 230°C/Fan 220°C/Gas 8. Line three large baking trays with baking parchment.

2 Spread the aubergine slices out on one lined baking tray. Lay the butternut squash slices on another tray and sprinkle with the chopped rosemary. Drizzle each tray of veg with 1 tbsp extra-virgin olive oil and season with salt and pepper. Cook in the oven for 20 minutes, then remove and set aside.

3 Lay the portobello mushrooms on the other baking tray, season with salt and pepper and drizzle with the remaining extra-virgin olive oil. Cook in the oven for 10 minutes, then remove and set aside. Turn the oven down to 200°C/Fan 180°C/Gas 6.

4 While the veg are in the oven, prepare the tomato sauce. Heat the olive oil in a large saucepan over a medium heat. Add the chopped onion and cook for 7–10 minutes, until softened. Add the garlic and cook for another 2 minutes. Sprinkle in the dried oregano.

5 Stir in the tinned tomatoes, passata and water, then season with salt and pepper to taste. Bring to the boil, lower the heat and simmer for 15 minutes until the sauce is reduced and thickened.

6 While the tomato sauce is thickening, make the cheese sauce. Melt the butter into a large non-stick saucepan over a medium heat. Add the flour and stir with a wooden spoon over a medium-low heat for 2–3 minutes. Gradually stir in the milk and bring to

Continued overleaf

a gentle simmer. Swap the spoon for a whisk and begin to whisk the sauce as it starts to thicken.

7 Add the grated nutmeg, half the Cheddar and half the Parmesan to the sauce. Tear one of the mozzarella balls into small pieces, add these to the sauce and stir until melted, then remove from the heat.

8 Spread a few ladlefuls of tomato sauce evenly in the bottom of a large roasting dish, about 38 x 27cm and 8cm deep. Cover with a layer of lasagne sheets. Add a layer of aubergine and courgette, along with a ladleful of tomato sauce, then spoon on a ladleful of cheese sauce. Cover with a layer of lasagne sheets.

9 Now add a layer of roasted peppers and artichokes along with a ladleful of tomato sauce. Tear one ball of mozzarella into this layer and add a little cheese sauce, then a layer of lasagne sheets.

10 Follow with a layer of mushrooms and cavolo nero, then finish with the roasted squash, adding some tomato sauce, cheese sauce and a layer of lasagne sheets, as before.

11 Tear over the remaining ball of mozzarella and cover with a final layer of lasagne sheets. Spread the rest of the cheese sauce evenly over the top. Scatter over the remaining Cheddar and Parmesan and bake in the oven for 45–50 minutes.

12 Remove the lasagne from the oven and leave to rest for 5 minutes before serving.

To freeze: Allow to cool, then freeze in two-portion lidded foil trays. Defrost fully in the fridge overnight. Cover loosely with foil and reheat in an oven preheated to 200°C/Fan 180°C/Gas 6 for 30 minutes, or until piping hot.

Mushroom and truffle mac 'n' cheese

This is a super-indulgent macaroni cheese to brighten up midweek mealtimes. The truffle and porcini paste makes it taste very luxurious, without the expense of buying fresh truffles! ♡ ❋

BATCH COOKING

Serves 8
550 calories per serving

750g dried macaroni
Sea salt and freshly ground black pepper

For the cheese sauce
100g butter
100g plain flour
1.25 litres skimmed milk
½ nutmeg, finely grated
2 x 80g jars truffle and porcini paste
1 tbsp porcini mushroom powder
100g reduced-fat strong Cheddar, grated
50g Parmesan, finely grated
125g ball reduced-fat mozzarella, torn into pieces

For the mushrooms
2 tbsp butter
1 tbsp olive oil
500g chestnut mushrooms, sliced
3 garlic cloves, sliced
2 tbsp thyme leaves

For the topping
100g fresh breadcrumbs
50g Parmesan, finely grated
2 tbsp finely chopped flat-leaf parsley

1 To make the cheese sauce, melt the butter in a large non-stick saucepan over a medium heat. Add the flour and cook, stirring with a wooden spoon, over a medium-low heat for 2–3 minutes. Gradually stir in the milk and bring to a gentle simmer.

2 Swap the spoon for a whisk and whisk until the sauce begins to thicken. Add the nutmeg, truffle and porcini paste, mushroom powder and all three cheeses. Stir until the cheeses have melted into the sauce, then remove from the heat. Season with salt and pepper to taste.

3 Preheat the oven to 200°C/Fan 180°C/Gas 6. Bring a large pan of salted water to the boil. Add the macaroni and cook for 8–10 minutes or until *al dente*.

4 In the meantime, to cook the mushrooms, melt the butter with the olive oil in a frying pan over a high heat. Add the mushrooms and cook, stirring occasionally, for 10 minutes. Add the garlic and thyme leaves and cook for another 2–3 minutes.

5 Drain the macaroni, keeping back some of the cooking water. Mix the macaroni with the cheese sauce and cooked mushrooms. If the mixture is too thick, loosen it with a little of the reserved cooking water. Season with salt and pepper to taste.

6 Spoon into a large oven dish, about 35 x 25cm and 8cm deep. Sprinkle the breadcrumbs and Parmesan evenly over the surface then bake on the middle shelf of the oven for 10 minutes. Turn the grill on and cook

for a further 5 minutes until golden brown, keeping a close eye on the topping to make sure it doesn't burn.

7 Serve in warmed bowls, sprinkled with chopped parsley and accompanied by a green salad, if you like.

To freeze: Let cool at the end of step 5, then freeze in two-portion lidded foil trays. Defrost fully in the fridge overnight. Remove lids. If it's a bit stodgy after thawing, add a splash of milk. Sprinkle with the topping and cook as above in the oven at 200°C/Fan 180°C/Gas 6, allowing an extra 10 minutes before turning the grill on.

FOOD IS ALL ABOUT enjoyment, so what better way to spend the weekend than by inviting a few friends over and cooking up a feast? Choose recipes that you know you'll have fun with and don't worry about aiming for perfection. There is nothing nicer than being cooked for, and everyone will be so pleased to be off duty that they won't even notice if it hasn't turned out quite as you had planned.

For a simple twist on your regular Sunday roast, why not try my Chicken with roasted cauliflower on page 198? It has a great flavour and it's all cooked in one tray, so there's minimal washing up. Or for a relaxed weekend treat that is ready in about half an hour, the chicken burger on page 201 is a real crowd-pleaser and has an amazing ranch dressing that brings back childhood memories. For those times when you're up for something a bit fancier, try the spiced sea bass on page 212. The flavours are delicate and it looks impressive, but it's still easy to put together.

The beauty of cooking at the weekend is that you have a little more time on your hands. With that in mind, I've included lots of recipes that cook 'low and slow', such as Middle Eastern slow-cooked lamb (page 192), Italian slow-cooked lamb ragu (page 197) and Slow-cooked beef brisket (page 206). The main advantage of this method is that the oven does all the hard work for you! That extra time allows flavours to develop slowly and with more depth, unlike the punchy hits of flavour that I usually aim for in quicker midweek cooking.

If midweek cooking can sometimes feel a bit rushed, these are the recipes to help you relax into your weekend cooking and really enjoy it – so have some fun creating lasting memories with some good food and great company.

Middle Eastern slow-cooked lamb

This fantastic alternative to your usual Sunday roast lamb is full of vibrant and bold Middle Eastern flavours, but it won't overpower with chilli heat. I serve it with tahini yoghurt and a crunchy, fresh salad with mint, watercress and pomegranate seeds.

Serves 8
720 calories per serving
815 calories with flatbreads

5 onions, peeled, topped, tailed and halved crossways
1 lamb shoulder joint (bone-in), about 2kg
2 tbsp baharat spice mix
4 garlic cloves, finely crushed
A handful of mint leaves, finely chopped
3 tbsp pomegranate molasses
2 tbsp olive oil
500ml lamb stock
Sea salt and freshly ground black pepper

For the salad
1 pomegranate, halved
2 cucumbers, peeled, halved lengthways, deseeded and thickly sliced
3 Little Gem lettuces, leaves separated
2 handfuls of watercress
2 handfuls of mint leaves, torn
2 tbsp extra-virgin olive oil
Juice of ½ lemon

For the tahini yoghurt
80g tahini
Juice of ½ lemon
200g Greek strained yoghurt (0% fat)

To serve
Sumac, for sprinkling
Flatbreads (optional)

1 Take the lamb out of the fridge an hour before cooking. Preheat the oven to 170°C/Fan 160°C/Gas 3.

2 Place the onions, cut side up, in the middle of a roasting tray. Using a sharp knife, make small incisions in the lamb shoulder about 2cm apart. Sit the lamb joint on top of the onions.

3 In a bowl, stir together the spice mix, garlic, mint, pomegranate molasses and olive oil and season well with salt and pepper. Drizzle the mixture over the lamb, rubbing it into the incisions as you do so. Pour the lamb stock into the roasting tray.

4 Cover the roasting tray with foil, folding it under the rim of the tray all round to seal. Cook in the oven for 3 hours. Remove the foil and baste the meat with the juices. Turn the oven up to 200°C/Fan 180°C/Gas 6 and roast the meat, uncovered, for 30 minutes.

5 For the salad, holding the pomegranate halves cut side down over a bowl, bash with a spoon to release the seeds into the bowl; pick out any membrane. Add all the remaining ingredients and toss to combine.

6 For the tahini yoghurt, mix the ingredients together and season with salt and pepper to taste.

7 Take the tray from the oven, cover the meat loosely with foil and leave to rest for 10–15 minutes. Carve the lamb and sprinkle with a little sumac. Serve with the roasted onions, tahini yogurt, salad and flatbreads. Spoon the pan juices over the meat too.

Greek-style roast lamb and potatoes

I am a huge fan of Greek cooking and for me this one-tray wonder conjures up memories of great summer holidays. The ingredients are very simple, allowing the individual flavours to really sing out. A classic Greek salad is the perfect complement.

Serves 8
805 calories per serving

2kg leg of lamb joint (bone-in)
3 garlic cloves, sliced
2kg potatoes, peeled and cut into large 5cm chunks
4 tbsp extra-virgin olive oil
1 tbsp dried Greek oregano
2 sprigs of rosemary, leaves picked and finely chopped
2 sprigs of oregano, leaves picked and chopped
Juice of 1 lemon
250ml lamb stock
Sea salt and freshly ground black pepper

For the Greek salad
1 red onion, diced
2 red peppers, cored, deseeded and diced
1 cucumber, halved lengthways and sliced
450g ripe tomatoes on the vine, cut into wedges
3 tbsp extra-virgin olive oil
2 tbsp red wine vinegar
½ tsp dried oregano
120g black olives
150g feta cheese, crumbled

1 Take the lamb out of the fridge about an hour before cooking, to bring it to room temperature.

2 Preheat the oven to 220°C/Fan 200°C/Gas 7. Using a sharp knife, make small incisions in the lamb, about 2cm apart. Push the garlic slices into the slits to flavour the meat.

3 Spread the potatoes out in the bottom of a large roasting tray. Drizzle with 2 tbsp of the extra-virgin olive oil and sprinkle with the dried oregano and some salt and pepper.

4 Mix together the rest of the olive oil, the chopped rosemary and oregano, lemon juice and a generous amount of salt and pepper.

5 Place the lamb in the roasting tray, in the middle of the potatoes, and drizzle the lemony oil over the top. Roast in the oven for 40 minutes, tossing the potatoes halfway through cooking.

6 Take the tray from the oven and lower the oven setting to 200°C/Fan 180°C/Gas 6 (leave the oven door open for a couple of minutes to help lower the temperature). Add the stock to the roasting tray.

7 Return the tray to the oven and roast for a further 30 minutes for medium to medium rare lamb. (On a temperature probe, it should register 51–55°C.) Baste the lamb with the juices and toss the potatoes once or twice during cooking. If you prefer lamb medium to well done, cook for a further 15 minutes.

8 In the meantime, to prepare the Greek salad, put all the salad veg into a large bowl, add the extra-virgin oil, wine vinegar, oregano and olives and toss to mix. Add the crumbled feta, toss gently and season with salt and pepper to taste.

9 Once the lamb is cooked, take the tray out of the oven. Transfer the meat to a warmed platter, cover loosely with foil and let rest for 20–30 minutes. Keep the potatoes warm, uncovered, in the turned-off oven. Carve the lamb and serve with the potatoes and salad.

Italian slow-cooked lamb ragu

This ragu has a wonderfully intense flavour. The longer you leave it, the better it will be as the lamb will become meltingly tender and flake easily, a bit like pulled pork. ❄

Serves 8
615–625 calories per serving

For the lamb ragu
2 tbsp olive oil
1.2kg boneless lamb shoulder, cut into 3.5cm cubes
2 onions, diced
3 carrots, peeled and diced
4 celery sticks, diced
4 garlic cloves, finely chopped
3 tbsp tomato purée
6 anchovy fillets in oil, drained
400ml red wine
4 sprigs of thyme
2 sprigs of rosemary
2 bay leaves
500ml lamb stock
2 x 400g tins chopped tomatoes
Sea salt and freshly ground black pepper

To serve
600–800g fresh pappardelle
Freshly grated Parmesan (optional)

1 Heat half the olive oil in a large non-stick casserole pan over a high heat. Season the lamb with salt and pepper and colour in batches in the hot oil until well browned on all sides; don't overcrowd the pan. Remove the lamb to a plate and set aside.

2 Preheat the oven to 170°C/Fan 160°C/Gas 3. Add the remaining oil to the pan, then the onions. Cook over a medium-high heat for 5 minutes to soften. Toss in the carrots, celery and garlic and cook for a further 8 minutes. Stir in the tomato purée and anchovies.

3 Pour in the wine, scraping up any sediment stuck to the bottom of the pan. Let it bubble until the liquid is reduced by half, 4–5 minutes. Add the herbs, lamb stock and tinned tomatoes and return the meat to the pan. Put the lid on and cook in the oven for 2 hours.

4 Take the casserole out of the oven, remove the lid, give it a good stir and then place the pan on the hob over a medium-low heat. Simmer gently for 1 hour to reduce and thicken the sauce. Remove any large herb sprigs. Flake the lamb with two forks in the casserole, then taste the ragu to check the seasoning.

5 Bring a pan of salted water to the boil. Add the pappardelle and cook for 2–3 minutes until *al dente*; drain well. Serve with the ragu and Parmesan, if you like.

To freeze the lamb ragu: Allow to cool, then freeze in two-portion containers. Defrost fully in the fridge overnight, then reheat in a saucepan over a medium heat, until hot right through. You may need to add a little extra liquid to loosen the ragu as you reheat it.

197

Chicken with roasted cauliflower

Full of flavour and with a great texture, roast cauliflower is the ideal partner for roast chicken. Chunks of toasted sourdough take the place of potatoes, providing a bit of crunch and soaking up all the lovely roasting juices.

Serves 6–8
615–820 calories per serving

1 large free-range chicken,
about 2.7kg
2 medium cauliflowers, trimmed,
leafy stalks retained
2 tbsp extra-virgin olive oil
2 garlic cloves, grated
2 tbsp lemon thyme leaves, chopped
1 crumbly chicken stock cube
300ml chicken stock
Sea salt and freshly ground black
pepper

For the toasted sourdough
300g sourdough bread, torn into
bite-sized pieces
1 tbsp extra-virgin olive oil
2 tbsp finely chopped flat-leaf
parsley

1 Take the chicken out of the fridge 30 minutes before you want to cook it. Preheat the oven to 170°C/Fan 150°C/Gas 3.

2 Lay the leafy stalks from the cauliflowers in a large roasting tray (to sit the chicken on). Set the cauliflower heads aside.

3 In a small bowl, mix the extra-virgin olive oil with the garlic, chopped thyme and a little salt and pepper. Carefully insert your fingers under the skin of the chicken breasts and loosen the skin from the breasts. Push most of the olive oil mixture under the skin and spread it over the breast meat with your fingers. Sit the chicken on the cauliflower stalks.

4 Trickle the remaining olive oil mix over the surface of the chicken and rub in well with your hands. Season with pepper and crumble the stock cube evenly over. Cover the tray with foil and seal it to the rim of the tray all round. Cook for 1 hour and 20 minutes.

5 In the meantime, break the cauliflower into florets. When the time is up, take the tray from the oven and lift off the foil. Turn the oven up to 220°C/Fan 200°C/Gas 7. While it is coming up to temperature, add the cauliflower florets to the roasting tray and pour in the chicken stock.

6 Place the tray on the bottom shelf of the oven. Roast for 30–40 minutes or until the chicken is golden brown all over and the cauliflower is cooked, basting the chicken with the juices halfway through.

7 For the toasted sourdough, 20 minutes before the end of the cooking time, scatter the sourdough chunks on a small baking tray. Drizzle with the 1 tbsp olive oil and season with salt and pepper. Place on the top shelf of the oven for 15–20 minutes or until golden brown.

8 Sprinkle the chopped parsley over the sourdough and mix well. Remove the chicken from the oven and leave to rest for 15 minutes before carving. Serve the chicken with the roasted cauliflower and toasted sourdough, spooning over the pan juices.

Chicken and bacon ranch burger

This easy chicken burger is ready in under half an hour. That's quicker than most takeaways and perfect for lazy weekend dining. It's the ranch dressing that really elevates this to the next level, though, balancing the saltiness of the bacon and adding a slight punch from the cayenne and hot sauce.

Serves 4
705 calories per serving

4 skinless, boneless chicken breasts
2 garlic cloves, grated
2 tbsp olive oil
8 rashers of smoked streaky bacon
4 large wholemeal burger buns
2 Little Gem lettuces, leaves
separated
2 large tomatoes, sliced
1 ripe avocado, quartered and sliced
Sea salt and freshly ground black
pepper

For the ranch dressing
2 tbsp reduced-fat mayonnaise
2 tbsp low-fat soured cream
½ garlic clove, finely grated
2 tbsp finely chopped dill
1 tbsp finely chopped chives
3 dashes of Worcestershire sauce
A pinch of cayenne pepper
2 dashes of Sriracha hot sauce
½ tsp white wine vinegar
1 tsp mild American mustard

1 Preheat the oven to 200°C/Fan 180°C/Gas 6. Line an oven tray with baking parchment.

2 On a clean board, bash each chicken breast with a rolling pin to a 1cm even thickness. Lay the chicken breasts in a shallow dish. Add the garlic, olive oil and some salt and pepper and rub well into the chicken. Set aside to marinate for 15 minutes.

3 Meanwhile, lay the bacon rashers on a wire rack over the lined oven tray. Cook in the oven for 12–15 minutes or until browned and crispy.

4 For the ranch dressing, mix all the ingredients together and season with salt and pepper to taste.

5 Heat a large griddle pan over a high heat. Cut the burger buns in half and toast the cut sides on the griddle in batches, until lightly charred. Set aside.

6 Lay the chicken breasts on the griddle and cook for 2–3 minutes on each side or until cooked through.

7 To assemble the burgers, spread 1 tbsp of ranch dressing over the bottom of each burger bun. Add the lettuce, chicken, tomato, bacon and avocado. Spread some more ranch dressing on the top half of the burger bun. Place on top of the filling and serve.

TIP ✔ The ranch dressing works just like barbecue sauce, balancing sweet with acidic. Try it next time you grill or barbecue steak, chops or sausages, or serve it as a dip for baked potato wedges (see page 102).

Chicken, ham and leek pie

Making a pie from scratch feels like an accomplishment, but it's not that hard. This hot water crust pastry is forgiving, too – easy to roll and move around. There's a lot going on in the pie, so serve it simply with boiled new potatoes or mash and a salad.

Serves 8
1055 calories per serving

3 bay leaves
1 tsp black peppercorns
5 sprigs of thyme
5 sprigs of rosemary
1 litre chicken stock
10 skinless, bone-in chicken thighs
2 leeks, trimmed, well washed and thickly sliced
80g unsalted butter
80g plain flour
50ml double cream
2 tbsp hot English mustard
50g mature Cheddar, grated
300g flaked, cooked smoked ham hock
2 tbsp flat-leaf parsley leaves, finely chopped
Sea salt and freshly ground white pepper

For the hot water crust pastry
750g plain flour
1 tsp salt
2 large free-range eggs, lightly beaten
125g unsalted butter, diced
125g lard, diced
250ml water
2 large free-range egg yolks, beaten with a pinch of salt, for glazing

1 Place the bay leaves, peppercorns, thyme and rosemary on a square of muslin, draw up the edges and tie tightly with kitchen string to enclose the flavourings. Place in a saucepan and pour on the chicken stock. Bring the stock to a simmer and allow to infuse over a low heat for 5 minutes.

2 Add the chicken thighs, bring back to a simmer and cook gently for 25 minutes. Add the leeks to the pan and cook for another 15 minutes until they are soft. Drain the chicken and leeks in a sieve over a heatproof bowl, to save the stock. When cool enough to handle, pull the chicken off the bones and set aside on a plate.

3 Melt the butter in a large saucepan over a medium-low heat, then add the flour and cook, stirring, for 1 minute to make a roux. Swap the spoon for a whisk. Slowly add 600ml of the reserved chicken stock to the roux, whisking constantly to keep the sauce smooth. (Save any remaining stock to use for soup, gravy etc.)

4 Continue cooking over a medium-low heat for 2–3 minutes, until the sauce thickens. Remove from the heat, add the cream, mustard and Cheddar and stir until the cheese has melted. Add the chicken, leeks, and flaked ham hock and season with salt and pepper to taste. Transfer to a large bowl, allow to cool, then stir through the chopped parsley. Refrigerate until needed.

5 To make the hot water crust pastry, place the flour and salt in the bowl of a stand mixer fitted with the

Continued overleaf

paddle attachment. Make a well in the centre and pour in the beaten eggs. Mix on a medium speed until well incorporated – the dough will be crumbly once the egg has been worked in.

6 Place the butter, lard and water in a small saucepan over a medium heat until the butter and lard have melted. Turn the mixer to a low speed and gradually pour in the hot liquid, stopping as soon as a dough forms; you may not need all the liquid. (Alternatively, you can mix the pastry by hand, using a wooden spoon to beat in the eggs, then the melted mixture.)

7 Take the dough out of the bowl and divide into two pieces, one twice the size of the other: one-third for your pie lid, and the larger portion to line the pie tin.

8 On a lightly floured surface, roll out the larger piece to a round, 5mm thick. Use to line the base and sides of a 23cm round non-stick pie tin, 5cm deep, pushing the pastry into the sides. Let the excess overhang the rim and brush the pastry on the rim with beaten egg yolk.

9 Roll out the other piece of pastry to a round, 5mm thick, for the pie lid. Spoon the cooled filling into the pastry-lined pie tin. Cover with the pastry lid and cut away the overhanging excess pastry from the edge. (There will be quite a lot of trimmings.) Press the edges together with your fingertips, to seal and crimp.

10 Brush the surface evenly with beaten egg yolk and cut a small hole in the middle of the top, to allow the steam to escape. Place in the fridge for 30 minutes to allow the pastry to set. Meanwhile, preheat the oven to 210°C/Fan 190°C/Gas 5–6.

11 Bake the pie in the oven for 35–45 minutes or until the pastry is golden and crisp. Leave to stand for about 10 minutes before slicing and serving.

Slow-cooked beef brisket

This is total no-stress cooking, as you don't need to worry about timing the meat precisely. The dry rub acts as a pre-seasoning, and leaving it for 24 hours allows the flavours to permeate right into the meat, so try to leave it for that long if you can. ❄

Serves 10
510 calories per serving

2kg boned and rolled beef brisket joint
10 small baking potatoes, washed but not peeled
Sea salt and freshly ground black pepper

For the dry rub
1½ tbsp hot smoked paprika
2 tbsp ground cumin
2 tbsp ground coriander
1 tbsp dried thyme

For the sauce
200ml apple cider vinegar
100ml maple syrup
200ml ale
150ml tomato ketchup
300ml beef stock
2 tbsp Dijon mustard
1 tbsp Worcestershire sauce

For the coleslaw
½ red cabbage, sliced (300g)
½ white cabbage, sliced (300g)
1 large red onion, sliced
100g pickled chillies, chopped
1 tsp salt
3 tbsp Greek yoghurt (0% fat)
3 tbsp reduced-fat mayonnaise
3 tbsp roughly chopped parsley

1 For the dry rub, mix all the ingredients together in a small bowl. Place the beef in a non-metallic dish and rub the dry spice mixture all over the surface. Cover with cling film and leave to marinate in the fridge for 24 hours.

2 When ready to cook, preheat the oven to 150°C/Fan 140°C/Gas 2. Place the beef joint in a roasting tin. Put the potatoes on a baking tray and sprinkle with salt.

3 For the sauce, whisk all the ingredients together in a bowl and pour over the beef. Cover with foil, sealing the edges to the tin all round, and cook for 6 hours, or until the beef is tender. A couple of hours before the meat will be ready, put the potatoes into the oven.

4 Meanwhile, for the coleslaw, put all the ingredients into a large bowl and toss well. Taste for seasoning, adding pepper and a little more salt if needed.

5 To check that the beef is cooked, scrape it gently with a fork; it should fall apart. Remove from the oven and set it aside to rest for 15–20 minutes.

6 To serve, pull the meat apart, using two forks. Serve with the sauce spooned over and the baked potatoes and coleslaw on the side.

To freeze leftover beef: Leave the meat and juices to cool then freeze in one- or two-portion lidded foil trays. Defrost fully in the fridge overnight. Cover loosely with foil, and reheat in an oven preheated to 200°C/Fan 180°C/Gas 6 for 30–35 minutes or until piping hot.

Swedish meatballs

These are fun to make with kids – get them shaping and rolling the meatballs and helping with the mash. Note that they are roasted rather than fried, to lower the fat. Lingonberry sauce is exceptionally good with the meatballs, if you can find it.

Serves 4
760 calories per serving

1 tbsp olive oil
1 onion, finely chopped
500g lean beef mince (5% fat)
½ tsp freshly ground white pepper
½ tsp ground allspice
1 tsp garlic powder
50g fresh white breadcrumbs
1 large free-range egg, lightly beaten
2 tbsp finely chopped dill, plus extra to finish
3 tbsp flat-leaf parsley, finely chopped, plus extra to finish
1 tbsp cornflour
350ml beef stock
1 tbsp Worcestershire sauce
1 tsp Dijon mustard
150ml reduced-fat soured cream
Sea salt and freshly ground black pepper

For the mash
800g potatoes, peeled and cut into small chunks
2 tbsp unsalted butter
150ml reduced-fat soured cream

To serve
300g green beans, steamed

1 Preheat the oven to 250°C/Fan 240°C/Gas 10. Line a large baking tray with baking parchment.

2 Heat the olive oil in a non-stick frying pan over a medium-high heat, add the onion and sauté for about 10 minutes, until starting to turn golden brown, stirring frequently. Remove from the heat.

3 For the mash, put the potatoes into a large pan and pour on enough cold water to cover them by 5cm. Add a good pinch of salt. Bring to the boil, lower the heat slightly and simmer until tender, about 10–15 minutes.

4 Meanwhile, in a bowl, combine the mince, cooked onion, spices, breadcrumbs, egg and chopped herbs. Season generously with salt and pepper and mix well. Shape into 24 even-sized balls and place on the lined tray. Bake in the oven for 10 minutes, until browned.

5 Mix the cornflour with 2 tbsp beef stock. Pour the rest of the stock into a large frying pan set over a medium heat. Add the cornflour mix, Worcestershire sauce and mustard, whisking to combine. Add the meatballs and bring to a simmer. Simmer gently for 7–10 minutes, until the liquor is reduced by half. Remove from the heat and stir in the soured cream.

6 When the potatoes are cooked, drain them well and mash with the butter and soured cream. Season with salt and pepper to taste; keep warm. Serve the meatballs and sauce with the mash and green beans. Finish with chopped parsley and a grinding of pepper.

Spanish hake bake

You can't beat oven bakes like this for simplicity; they are such an easy and adaptable way of cooking. This healthy fish bake has lots of subtle flavours working together to produce a final dish that tastes fresh and clean. Serve it with lots of crusty bread to mop up the sauce.

Serves 4
490 calories per serving
625 calories with aïoli

4 skinless hake fillets, about 200g each
800g potatoes, peeled and thickly sliced
1 large white onion, very thinly sliced
1 medium fennel bulb, tough outer layer removed, very thinly sliced (about 200g prepared weight)
400ml vegetable stock
A large pinch of saffron strands
400g cherry tomatoes
80g green olives
Sea salt and freshly ground black pepper

To serve
2 tbsp flat-leaf parsley, finely chopped
1 lemon, for zesting
2 tbsp extra-virgin olive oil
Aïoli (good-quality shop-bought)

1 Preheat the oven to 220°C/Fan 200°C/Gas 7. Check the hake fillets for any pin-bones.

2 Put the potatoes into a large pan and add enough water to cover by 5cm. Bring to the boil, lower the heat and simmer for 5 minutes. Drain the potatoes and lay them in the bottom of an ovenproof dish (about 28cm in diameter and 7.5cm deep).

3 Scatter the onion and fennel slices in an even layer over the potatoes. Pour on the stock and sprinkle on the saffron and a little salt and pepper. Cover with foil and bake in the oven for 15 minutes.

4 Take the dish out of the oven and add the cherry tomatoes. Re-cover with foil and return to the oven for 8 minutes.

5 Take the dish from the oven and remove the foil. Season the fish fillets on both sides with salt and pepper and lay them on top of the vegetables. Add the olives and baste the fish with the saffron stock. Return to the oven, uncovered, and bake for 8 minutes.

6 Sprinkle with chopped parsley, zest over the lemon and drizzle with the extra-virgin olive oil. Serve with aïoli on the side, and provide crusty bread to mop up the delicious juices if you like.

TIP ✔ If you can't get hold of hake, use another meaty white fish, such as cod or haddock.

Spiced sea bass with roasted cauliflower purée and lentils

This is an impressive dish to serve if you are entertaining. Sea bass is a fairly robust fish, so it takes spices well. Here, it is complemented beautifully by the creamy cauliflower purée and spiced lentils. Place the fish whole in the centre of the table and let everyone help themselves.

Serves 6
775 calories per serving

2 sea bass, about 700g each, gutted and cleaned
Sea salt and freshly ground black pepper

For the roasted cauliflower purée
1.35kg cauliflower, stalk and leaves removed
2 tbsp olive oil
50g butter
250ml whipping cream
250ml semi-skimmed milk

For the sea bass marinade
4 garlic cloves, grated
5cm piece of fresh ginger, finely grated
2 tsp ground turmeric
2 tsp ground cumin
2 handfuls of coriander leaves
2 tbsp olive oil
120g natural yoghurt (0% fat)

For the spiced lentils
1 tbsp vegetable oil
1 onion, finely diced
1 tsp medium Madras curry powder
2 x 250g packs cooked Puy lentils
200ml vegetable stock
120g baby spinach

To finish
A handful of coriander leaves, torn

1 Preheat the oven to 220°C/Fan 200°C/Gas 7. Line two large baking trays with baking parchment.

2 For the cauliflower purée, cut the cauliflower into florets and spread them out on one lined baking tray. Drizzle with the olive oil and season with salt. Roast in the oven for 40 minutes or until golden brown, tossing halfway through.

3 Meanwhile, for the marinade, mix all the ingredients together in a small bowl, adding some salt and pepper. Using a sharp knife, score the fish on both sides on an angle, making 3 slashes on each side. Lay the fish on the other baking tray. Spread the marinade evenly all over the fish and leave to marinate for 20 minutes.

4 To make the cauliflower purée, melt the butter in a large frying pan over a medium heat. Add the roasted cauliflower florets and cook for 10 minutes or until well browned. Pour in the cream and milk and simmer for 7–10 minutes until reduced and thickened. Tip the contents of the pan into a blender and blitz until smooth. Return the purée to the pan; keep warm.

5 For the spiced lentils, heat the oil in a large frying pan, add the onion and cook over a medium heat for 7–10 minutes, until softened.

6 Meanwhile, place the tray of fish on the top shelf of the oven and cook for 15 minutes.

7 Stir the curry powder into the softened onion and cook for 30 seconds, then add the lentils. Pour in the vegetable stock and simmer for 5 minutes, until the liquid has reduced by half. Stir through the spinach and cook for 2 minutes, until it has wilted.

8 Once the fish is cooked, remove from the oven and run a cook's blowtorch over the skin to crisp it. Leave to rest for a few minutes. Serve the fish on a platter, scattered with the coriander and with the cauliflower purée and spiced lentils in warmed bowls alongside.

North African style nut roast

A delicious veggie Sunday lunch, this nut roast is full of flavour and has a great chunky texture. Combining heat and refreshing coolness, the lovely harissa yoghurt can be served alongside all kinds of meat and veggie dishes. (Jars of rose harissa can be found in the supermarket spice section.) ♡

Serves 8
390 calories per serving

600g peeled, deseeded butternut squash, cut into 2cm dice
3 tbsp olive oil
1 onion, diced
2 aubergines, diced
1 red pepper, cored, deseeded and diced
2 garlic cloves, sliced
3 tbsp ras el hanout
1 tbsp rose harissa
400g tin chickpeas, drained
170g bulgur wheat (dry weight), cooked
100g flaked almonds, toasted
Sea salt and freshly ground black pepper

For the harissa yoghurt
250g Greek strained yoghurt (0% fat)
2 tbsp rose harissa

For the parsley salad
3 handfuls of flat-leaf parsley leaves
50g baby leaf salad
1 red onion, finely sliced
1 tbsp pomegranate molasses
1 tbsp extra-virgin olive oil
Juice of ½ lemon

1 Preheat the oven to 200°C/Fan 180°C/Gas 6. Grease a 1.25kg (3lb) loaf tin and line with baking parchment. Line a baking tray with parchment.

2 Place the diced squash on the baking tray, season with salt and pepper and trickle over 1 tbsp olive oil. Roast in the oven for 30 minutes or until softened.

3 Meanwhile, heat the remaining olive oil in a large non-stick frying pan over a medium-high heat. Add the onion and aubergines and sauté for 10 minutes or until softened and brown. Add the red pepper and garlic and cook for 5 minutes. Stir in the ras el hanout and harissa and cook for 2 minutes. Take off the heat.

4 Using a food processor and the pulse button, briefly blitz half the squash and half the aubergine mix with the chickpeas until chunky but not puréed.

5 Transfer to a large bowl and add the remaining squash, aubergine, cooked bulgur wheat and almonds. Mix well and season generously with salt and pepper. Pack into the prepared loaf tin and bake for 1 hour.

6 Meanwhile, mix the yoghurt and harissa together in a bowl and season with salt and pepper to taste. For the parsley salad, toss all the ingredients together in a bowl and season with salt and pepper.

7 Once cooked, remove the nut roast from the oven and leave in the tin for 20 minutes, then turn out on to a board. Cut into 8 slices, using a serrated knife, and serve with the parsley salad and harissa yoghurt.

DESSERTS ARE GREAT for enticing tentative cooks into the kitchen. Eating well is all about balance after all, and who can resist a slightly gooey chocolate chip cookie straight from the oven, or stop themselves going to investigate the smell of spiced apple crumble wafting around the house? Getting started in the kitchen is often the hardest part, and if puddings help you get there, then that's fine! From baking sweet things, you can then move on to the other, healthier recipes in this book – and take the rest of the family with you.

Sweet treats are also a fun way for children to learn about cooking. They can help with weighing and measuring out the ingredients, and then give you a hand with mixing and pouring, and licking the bowl! If you set aside an hour or so to bake a cake together on a Sunday, you'll be helping to create some really positive memories.

If you're used to buying mass-produced cakes, puddings and biscuits, then my recipes are always going to be better for you, because they are made from proper ingredients and have minimal added sugar. There are lots of fruit-based sweet things too – from Banana and berry nice cream (page 226) and Plum and ginger fool (page 231) to Caribbean rum pineapple (228) and Apricot, date and pistachio flapjacks (page 247). There's even a chocolate cake that includes beetroot on page 256; it has a wonderfully rich texture and an amazing colour.

Sometimes puddings are about pure decadent celebration, and for those occasions I suggest you skip straight to the rich Chocolate truffle tart (page 232), Sticky date pudding with coconut caramel (page 240) or Chocolate and peanut butter brownies (page 244). These are unashamedly luxurious, and I reckon anyone you make them for will immediately want to make them too. Food is there to be enjoyed and there's nothing wrong with the odd treat once in a while, especially if it tastes this good.

Yoghurt pannacotta with poached rhubarb

Rhubarb has a wonderful sharpness that works so well with dairy. Be careful not to overcook it, as you want it to retain a little bite to contrast with the creamy pannacotta.

Serves 6
315 calories per serving

4 sheets of leaf gelatine (fine-leaf, quick-dissolving)
150ml single cream
150ml whole milk
150g golden caster sugar
Finely pared zest of 1 lemon (removed in strips, with a vegetable peeler)
2 vanilla pods, split and seeds scraped
400g full-fat Greek yoghurt (8-10% fat), at room temperature

For the rhubarb topping
450g rhubarb, cut into 5cm lengths on an angle
40ml grenadine
Finely grated zest of ½ orange, plus 40ml orange juice
40ml water
40g golden caster sugar

To finish
20g unsalted pistachios, roughly chopped

1 Preheat the oven to 110°C/Fan 100°C/Gas ¼. Line a roasting tray with baking parchment.

2 Place the gelatine in a shallow dish, cover with cold water and leave to soak for 5 minutes or until soft.

3 Meanwhile, put the cream, milk, sugar, lemon zest and vanilla seeds into a small saucepan over a medium heat. Heat gently, stirring, until the sugar dissolves. Bring to a simmer and take off the heat. Immediately lift the gelatine out of the water and add it to the hot creamy milk, stirring until it has dissolved.

4 Pour the mixture into a large bowl, discarding the lemon zest. Leave to cool for 10 minutes, then whisk in the yoghurt and set aside to cool a little.

5 Pour the mixture evenly into 6 serving glasses (each 400ml capacity). Stand the glasses on a tray and place in the fridge for 2–3 hours to set.

6 Meanwhile, place the rhubarb in the lined roasting tray and spoon over the grenadine, orange juice and water. Sprinkle over the orange zest and sugar. Mix well, then spread the rhubarb out in a single layer. Cover the tray with foil and bake for about 50 minutes or until the rhubarb is just cooked. Remove from the oven and leave to cool in the tray.

7 To serve, top the set pannacottas with the cooled rhubarb and syrup from the baking tray. Sprinkle with chopped pistachios.

Quick chocolate mousse

I know it sounds a bit bizarre to use avocado in a dessert, but the rich creaminess is honestly fantastic. It results in a luxurious, rich mousse without needing to add loads of cream or sugar. ♡

Serves 8
380 calories per serving

2 ripe avocados, halved, stoned and peeled (prepared weight 190g)
2 ripe medium bananas (prepared weight 210g)
80g good-quality cocoa powder
2 tbsp vanilla extract
1 tsp orange extract
Finely grated zest of 1 orange
120ml maple syrup
10 Medjool dates, chopped
100ml milk

To finish
40g good-quality dark chocolate (70% cocoa solids)
50g pecans, toasted and chopped
50g macadamia nuts, toasted and chopped
1 tsp sea salt flakes

1 Put the avocado flesh into a food processor and add the bananas, breaking them into pieces. Add the cocoa powder, vanilla and orange extracts, orange zest, maple syrup, dates and milk. Blend until smooth.

2 Spoon the mousse evenly into glass bowls and grate chocolate over each portion. Sprinkle with the chopped nuts and sea salt flakes to serve.

Strawberry Eton mess

This pretty and colourful pudding is a fun one to assemble with kids. You really don't have to worry about what the end result looks like, so get everyone involved layering up the fruit, meringues and cream, and scattering over the nuts. ∨

Serves 4
645 calories per serving

For the meringues
2 large free-range egg whites
115g caster sugar

For the strawberries
600g strawberries, hulled and
    quartered
2 tbsp elderflower cordial
3 tbsp caster sugar
1 tbsp water

For the vanilla cream
400ml whipping cream
1 vanilla pod, split and seeds
    scraped
400g Greek yoghurt (0% fat)

For the mint sugar
A handful of mint leaves
50g demerara sugar

To finish
Unsalted pistachios, chopped

1 Preheat the oven to 110°C/Fan 100°C/Gas ¼. Line two baking sheets with non-stick silicone mats or baking parchment.

2 To make the meringues, put the egg whites into a very clean, large bowl. Using an electric whisk on a medium speed, beat until stiff peaks form when the beaters are lifted. Sprinkle in half the sugar and beat well for 1–2 minutes. Gradually beat in the remaining sugar. Once it is all incorporated, beat for another 2 minutes or until the mixture is thick and glossy.

3 Transfer the meringue to a piping bag fitted with a 1.5cm plain piping nozzle. Pipe about 50 rounds (no more than 2.5cm in diameter) onto the prepared baking sheets, spacing them evenly and leaving a little peak in the middle of each as you lift the nozzle. Bake for 1 hour, then turn the oven off. Leave the meringues inside for a further hour with the door closed. Take the meringues out and set aside until cold.

4 Meanwhile, put 350g of the strawberries into a bowl and spoon on the elderflower cordial. Stir well and set aside to macerate.

5 Put the remaining 250g strawberries into a small pan with the sugar and water. Bring to a simmer over a medium heat and simmer gently for 8–10 minutes until the strawberries are softened. Leave to cool, then blitz using a small food processor until smooth.

6 For the vanilla cream, whip the cream in a bowl until thick, then fold in the vanilla seeds and yoghurt. Swirl

through half the strawberry purée, then crumble in half of the meringues. Stir gently to just combine.

7 For the mint sugar, blitz the mint leaves and sugar in a small food processor until the mixture looks like a green crumble.

8 Divide half of the remaining meringues between 4 serving bowls. Spoon on half of the vanilla cream mix, macerated strawberries and strawberry purée. Repeat these layers and finish with a sprinkle of mint sugar and chopped pistachios.

Banana and berry nice cream

The perfect solution for those over-ripe bananas sitting in your fruit bowl! This is an easy, almost instant ice cream that tastes sweet and rich, even though it doesn't contain any added sugar or cream. ♡ ❄

Serves 4
210 calories per serving

3 ripe medium bananas, peeled (about 300g peeled weight)
300g mixed frozen berries
100ml coconut milk
4 tbsp maple syrup
30g flaked almonds, toasted
50g dried cranberries

1 Thickly slice the bananas and freeze on a tray until firm.

2 Place the frozen bananas, berries, coconut milk and maple syrup in a food processor and blend until smooth. If you aren't ready to eat it straight away, place in a container and pop it in the freezer for later.

3 Spoon the ice cream into bowls and top with flaked almonds and cranberries. (Alternatively, you can serve it in waffle ice-cream cones.)

TIP ✔ If you have bananas over-ripening in the fruit bowl but don't want to turn them into a 'nice cream' straight away, peel, slice and freeze them on a tray until firm, then pack into a freezer container. Keep frozen until needed.

Caribbean rum pineapple

Pineapple has such a sweet, heady flavour, it can handle spices well. Ginger biscuits add a contrasting crunch and an extra layer of flavour to this decadent dessert. ♡

Serves 8
480 calories per serving

1 large pineapple
120g light brown sugar
½ tsp ground cinnamon
½ tsp ground allspice
100ml dark rum
1 vanilla pod, split and seeds scraped
50g butter

For the ginger nut biscuits
50g butter, softened
75g light brown sugar
4 tbsp golden syrup
175g plain flour, plus extra for dusting
½ tsp bicarbonate of soda
2 tsp ground ginger

To serve
500ml coconut ice cream (shop-bought)
25g coconut flakes, toasted
1 lime, for zesting

1   To prepare the pineapple, slice off the top and bottom, then stand it on a board and slice off the skin, removing the 'eyes' too. Turn the pineapple on its side and cut into 6–8 thick rounds. Remove the core from each round, using a small plain cutter or a small, sharp knife. Lay the pineapple slices in a shallow tray.

2   Put the sugar, cinnamon, allspice, rum, vanilla seeds and butter into a small saucepan and stir over a medium heat for about 5 minutes, until the butter is melted and the sugar dissolved. Pour this syrup over the pineapple and leave to macerate for 30 minutes.

3   Preheat the oven to 190°C/Fan 170°C/Gas 5. Line two baking sheets with baking parchment.

4   To make the ginger nut biscuits, beat the butter and sugar together in a large bowl until light and fluffy. Add the golden syrup and beat until evenly combined. Sift the flour, bicarbonate of soda and ground ginger together over the mixture and mix briefly until it just comes together to form a dough.

5   Transfer the dough to a lightly floured surface and roll out to a 3mm thickness. Using a 6cm plain cutter, cut out 20 rounds and lay on the lined baking sheets. Bake for 10–12 minutes, rotating the trays and swapping them over on the shelves halfway through cooking. Remove and leave to cool on the trays.

6   When ready to serve, heat a griddle pan over a medium heat. Lift the pineapple slices out of the marinade onto a plate. Pour the marinade into a small saucepan and bring to a simmer over a high heat.

Lower the heat to medium and let the sauce simmer gently for 3–5 minutes, until slightly thickened.

7 Cook the pineapple rings on the hot griddle, in batches if necessary, for 2–3 minutes on each side or until charred on both sides.

8 Lay a griddled pineapple slice on each serving plate and place a scoop of ice cream in the middle. Drizzle over the sauce and crumble a ginger nut or two over each plate. Sprinkle with toasted coconut flakes and zest a little lime over each portion. Serve at once.

Plum and ginger fool

If you have fruit that needs using up, turn it into a creamy, light fool for an easy pud. You could happily use strawberries or raspberries in place of plums and ginger. ∨

Serves 8
640 calories per serving

12 ripe plums, halved and stoned
4 balls of stem ginger in syrup,
**   finely chopped, plus 4 tbsp syrup**
**   from the jar**
50ml water
100g caster sugar
600ml whipping cream
600g Greek yoghurt (0% fat)

For the almond crumble topping
100g plain flour
80g golden caster sugar
80g cold butter, diced
1 tsp almond extract
80g flaked almonds, roughly
**   chopped**

1 Preheat the oven to 200°C/Fan 180°C/Gas 6. Line a baking tray with baking parchment.

2 Put the plums, chopped stem ginger and syrup, water and sugar into a large saucepan over a medium-high heat. Bring to a gentle boil, then lower the heat and simmer gently for 15–20 minutes or until the plums are softened and tender. Leave to cool slightly.

3 Meanwhile, for the topping, put the flour and sugar into a large bowl, add the butter and rub in with your fingers until the mixture resembles breadcrumbs. Add the almond extract and chopped almonds and mix well.

4 Spread the crumb mix out on the baking tray and place on the top shelf of the oven for 10–12 minutes or until golden and crunchy. Remove from the oven, break up any clumps with a wooden spoon and set aside to cool completely.

5 Tip the plum mixture into a blender and blitz until smooth. Set aside to cool completely.

6 Whip the cream in a large bowl until soft peaks form and then fold through the yoghurt; set aside one-third. Add half of the plum purée to the remaining two-thirds of the creamy yoghurt and fold through lightly.

7 Spoon half of the creamy plum mixture evenly into 6 serving glasses. Spoon on the remaining creamy yoghurt, then top with the rest of the creamy plum mix. Drizzle the remaining plum purée over the top. Place on a tray in the fridge to chill and firm up a little.

8 Scatter the crumble on top of the fools to serve.

Chocolate truffle tart

Hidden inside each luscious slice of this gooey tart is at least one chocolate truffle, waiting to be discovered. It is pure chocolate indulgence! ♡

For the chocolate pastry
250g plain flour
100g icing sugar
50g cocoa powder
200g butter, softened
2 large free-range egg yolks,
    beaten with 1 tbsp water

For the chocolate fondant filling
20 milk chocolate truffles with
    a solid centre (shop-bought)
125g unsalted butter
125g good-quality dark chocolate
    (70% cocoa solids), broken into
    pieces
4 large free-range eggs
115g caster sugar
40g plain flour

To finish
Cocoa powder, for dusting
About 150g crème fraîche
200–250g strawberries, halved
    or quartered if large

1   To make the pastry, using a stand mixer fitted with the paddle attachment, mix the flour, icing sugar, cocoa and butter together on a low speed until the mixture resembles breadcrumbs. Gradually add the beaten egg yolk mix until the mixture comes together to form a dough; you might not need all of it.

2   Shape the dough into a round, flatten to a disc and wrap in cling film. Place in the fridge to rest for 1 hour. Meanwhile, put the truffles for the fondant into the freezer to firm up.

3   On a lightly floured surface, roll out the dough to a 3mm thickness; it will still be very soft. Line the base of a 25cm non-stick tart tin with the pastry, pushing it into the edges. Place in the fridge for 30 minutes. Preheat the oven to 190°C/Fan 170°C/Gas 5.

4   Prick the base of the pastry case with a fork, then line with baking parchment and fill with baking beans. Place on a baking sheet in the oven and bake 'blind' for 15 minutes. Lift out the paper and beans and bake for a further 10 minutes to dry the base. Leave to cool.

5   To make the fondant, put the butter and chocolate into a heatproof bowl set over a pan of simmering water; make sure the base of the bowl doesn't touch the water. Stir gently over a low heat until melted.

6   Using the stand mixer fitted with the whisk attachment, whisk the eggs and sugar until light and fluffy. Pour in the melted chocolate and sift over the flour. Using a rubber spatula, gently fold everything together until just combined.

7 Pour half of the chocolate fondant into the pastry case. Arrange 12 truffles around the edge of the filling, spacing them evenly. Put the remaining truffles in the centre. Pour on the rest of the fondant and place in the fridge to chill for 30 minutes.

8 Bake the tart for 25 minutes or until the fondant is just set. Remove from the oven and let cool slightly. Sift a little cocoa powder over the tart, then remove from the tin and cut into 12 slices. Serve with a spoonful of crème fraîche and some strawberries.

White chocolate crack and raspberries

This is a play on something we make at The Hand and Flowers and it is always a big hit with our guests. Caramelising the chocolate in the oven on a low heat brings out its sweetness, adding rich undertones and a slight biscuity texture at the same time. Scattered over fresh berries, a little goes a long way. ♡

Serves 6
225 calories per serving

200g bar Belgian white chocolate
600g raspberries
200g Greek yoghurt (0% fat)

1　Preheat the oven to 170°C/Fan 150°C/Gas 3. Line a small baking tray with a non-stick silicone mat or baking parchment.

2　Place the bar of chocolate in the middle of the baking tray. Cook on the middle shelf of the oven for 15–20 minutes or until the chocolate has melted and caramelised evenly to a light golden brown colour. There will be tiny cracks over the surface.

3　Remove from the oven and immediately transfer the chocolate to a cold baking tray. Put it straight into the freezer for 15 minutes or until completely cold.

4　Divide the raspberries between 6 serving plates and add a generous dollop of yoghurt to each plate. Roughly break up the cooled chocolate and scatter over the raspberries to serve.

Crêpe Suzette cake

This is a real showstopper! It takes a little while to make, but the stages aren't all that complicated and it is well worth the effort. You can make the pancakes and custard the day before, leaving just the meringue, caramel and layering up to do. ♡

12 slices
455 calories per slice

For the custard
300ml whole milk
1 vanilla pod, split and seeds scraped
Finely grated zest of 1 orange
6 large free-range egg yolks (save 3 whites for the meringue)
100g caster sugar
2 tbsp cornflour
350g mascarpone

For the crêpe batter
165g plain flour
3 large free-range eggs
300ml whole milk
150ml water
75g butter, melted

For the orange caramel
50g caster sugar
1 tbsp water
Juice of 1 orange (60ml)
1 tbsp orange liqueur, such as Grand Marnier

For the Italian meringue
3 large free-range egg whites
165g caster sugar
45ml water

To finish
40g hazelnuts, toasted and roughly chopped
1 orange, for zesting

1 To make the custard, pour the milk into a saucepan and add the vanilla seeds and orange zest. Bring to a simmer over a low heat. Meanwhile, whisk the egg yolks, sugar and cornflour together in a large bowl. Pour on the hot milk, whisking as you do so. Pour back into the pan and stir over a low heat until the custard comes to a gentle simmer and thickens. Pour into a cold bowl, cover the surface with cling film and place in the fridge.

2 For the crêpe batter, put the flour into a large bowl, make a well in the centre and crack in the eggs. Whisk gently to combine, then whisk in the milk and water. Lastly whisk in 4 tbsp of the melted butter. Leave the batter to rest in the fridge for 30 minutes.

3 When the custard is cold, whisk in the mascarpone until smooth and then return to the fridge to chill.

4 To cook the crêpes, heat a 25cm non-stick crêpe pan over a high heat. Dip a folded piece of kitchen paper into the melted butter then wipe it over the base of the crêpe pan to coat it in a thin layer of butter.

5 Pour a ladleful of batter into the pan and tilt the pan to swirl the batter around and coat the base evenly. Cook for 1–2 minutes until golden on the underside, then flip the crêpe over using a spatula and cook for 1 minute on the other side. Transfer to a plate.

6 Repeat to cook the rest of the batter, making 12 crêpes in total, stacking them on the plate as they are cooked, interleaved with baking parchment to stop them sticking. Refrigerate to cool completely.

7 For the caramel, in a small heavy-based saucepan over a medium heat, dissolve the sugar in the water, swirling the pan to help the process. Increase the heat to high and cook the syrup to a golden caramel. Take off the heat. Immediately and carefully add the orange juice and liqueur (it will bubble up). Stir over a low heat for about 10 minutes, until you have a smooth, liquid caramel. Remove from the heat and let cool slightly.

8 To assemble, layer the crêpes up on a serving plate with a layer of custard in between each, leaving a 1cm clear margin at the edge, so the custard doesn't spill out. Refrigerate to set.

9 To make the Italian meringue, place the egg whites in the clean bowl of a stand mixer, fitted with the whisk attachment. Place 125g of the sugar and the water in a small saucepan and stir over a medium heat until the sugar dissolves. Increase the heat and cook until the sugar syrup registers 118°C on a sugar thermometer. At this point, with your mixer on full speed, whisk the egg whites until soft peaks form. Turn the speed to its lowest setting and sprinkle in the remaining 40g sugar. Whisk until combined and then switch off the mixer. Check your sugar syrup and remove it from the heat at 124°C. With the mixer turned on to its lowest setting again, slowly trickle in the sugar syrup, then increase the speed to high and whisk for a final 4–5 minutes.

10 Take the crêpe cake from the fridge and spoon the meringue evenly on top. Swirl with the back of a spoon and wave a cook's blowtorch over the surface to tinge the meringue golden brown. Drizzle with the orange caramel and scatter over the toasted hazelnuts and orange zest. Cut into slices and serve at once, drizzled with any remaining caramel.

Illustrated overleaf

Sticky date pudding with coconut caramel

I'm not going to pretend that this is healthy! It's a luxurious version of sticky toffee pudding, using coconut milk for the caramel sauce. It's about getting into the kitchen and making something to share with others... and they'll certainly thank you for it. ♡

Serves 12
545 calories per serving

A little butter or oil, for greasing
350g pitted dates, roughly chopped
250ml dark rum
300ml water
170g vegetable suet
200g light muscovado sugar
4 large free-range eggs
1 vanilla pod, split and seeds
**   scraped**
2 tsp ground mixed spice
400g self-raising flour
3 tsp bicarbonate of soda

For the coconut caramel
3 x 400ml tins coconut milk
100g light muscovado sugar

To finish
30g coconut flakes, toasted

1 Grease a 30 x 25cm baking tin, at least 5cm deep, and line with baking parchment.

2 Put the dates into a heatproof bowl. In a small pan, bring the rum and water to the boil, then pour over the dates. Stir, then cover and leave to soak for 20 minutes. Preheat the oven to 190°C/Fan 170°C/Gas 5.

3 Put the suet and sugar into a large bowl and stir to combine. Add the eggs, one at a time, mixing well after each addition. Add the vanilla and mixed spice to the bowl then sift over the flour and bicarbonate of soda; fold into the mixture until nearly combined. Add the dates with their liquor and mix to combine.

4 Pour the mixture into the prepared tin and bake on the middle shelf of the oven for 40 minutes or until a skewer inserted into the middle comes out with just a few moist crumbs clinging.

5 Meanwhile, to prepare the caramel, tip the coconut milk into a heavy-based non-stick saucepan and whisk until smooth. Bring to the boil over a high heat and boil rapidly, stirring occasionally, for about 40 minutes until reduced and starting to thicken. Sprinkle in the sugar and whisk well. (Reheat before serving if necessary.)

6 Once the pudding is cooked, remove from the oven and leave to stand for 5 minutes. Cut into squares and serve warm, trickled with hot coconut caramel and sprinkled with toasted coconut flakes.

Spiced apple crumble

As a nation, we're famous for our apples, but we don't seem to cook with them that often. This classic crumble includes two types: tart Bramleys, which break down to a smooth purée as they cook; and Granny Smiths, which stay firmer and introduce a slight sharpness. The nutty wholemeal topping adds an extra, almost salty flavour and a satisfying crunch. ♡ ❄

Serves 12
320 calories per serving
390 calories with ice cream

800g Bramley apples (about 2 large)
800g Granny Smith apples (about 4 large)
200ml water
30g butter
150g light muscovado sugar
100g sultanas
100g dates, roughly chopped
1 tsp ground ginger
1 tsp ground mixed spice
1 tsp ground cinnamon

For the crumble topping
80g wholemeal flour
100g cold butter, diced
100g rolled oats
50g pecans, finely chopped
50g walnuts, finely chopped
50g desiccated coconut

To serve
Vanilla ice cream (light, shop-bought)

1 Preheat the oven to 200°C/Fan 180°C/Gas 6.

2 Peel, quarter and core the apples, then chop into 2cm pieces, keeping them separate.

3 Put the Bramley apples into a large pan, along with the water and butter. Simmer gently for 10 minutes or until the apples begin to break down.

4 Add the Granny Smith apples, sugar, dried fruit and spices and cook for a further 10 minutes. Tip into a 25 x 30cm oven dish and spread out evenly.

5 For the crumble topping, put the flour into a bowl, add the butter and rub in with your fingertips until the mixture has a crumble texture. Tip in the rolled oats, chopped nuts and coconut and mix together until well combined.

6 Spread the crumble evenly over the top of the apples and cook on the middle shelf of the oven for 35–45 minutes or until the crumble is golden. Serve with ice cream (or you could have custard instead if you prefer).

To freeze: Allow the apple mixture to cool at the end of stage 4, then freeze in two-portion foil trays with cardboard lids. Defrost fully in the fridge overnight. Remove the lids, then scatter the topping over the apples and place in an oven preheated to 200°C/Fan 180°C/Gas 6 for 25–30 minutes until piping hot.

Chocolate and peanut butter brownies

Who can resist a brownie still a little warm from the oven? Peanut butter, swirled through the surface, introduces a salty-but-sweet flavour, a bit like salted caramel. The sweetness is offset by the dark chocolate, making this an all-round winner. ♡ ❄

Makes 12
390 calories per brownie

100g butter, plus extra for greasing
200g good-quality dark chocolate (70% cocoa solids), broken into pieces
150g smooth peanut butter
200g golden caster sugar
3 large free-range eggs
100g salted peanuts, roughly chopped
150g plain flour
1 tsp sea salt

1 Preheat the oven to 180°C/Fan 160°C/Gas 4. Lightly grease a 20cm square baking tin and line with baking parchment.

2 Put the chocolate into a heatproof bowl with the butter and 100g of the peanut butter. Stand the bowl over a pan of simmering water, making sure the base isn't touching the water, and stir until everything is melted. Remove from the heat, add the sugar and stir until it dissolves. Leave to cool slightly.

3 In a separate bowl, lightly whisk the eggs with a fork. Pour the eggs into the chocolate mixture and whisk until well combined.

4 Set aside a handful of the peanuts for the topping. Sift the flour over the melted chocolate mixture, then add the rest of the chopped peanuts and stir until just combined. Pour the mixture into the prepared tin.

5 Heat the remaining peanut butter in the microwave on a low setting (or in a small pan over a low heat) until softened. Drop teaspoonfuls onto the surface of the brownie and run a blunt knife through the mixture to swirl. Sprinkle over the reserved peanuts and sea salt.

6 Bake on the middle oven shelf for 25–30 minutes; it should still have a slight wobble in the middle as you take it out. Let cool slightly, then cut into squares. The brownies will keep for 3 days in an airtight container.

To freeze: Allow to cool completely then wrap in foil and seal in a plastic bag. Defrost at room temperature.

Apricot, date and pistachio flapjacks

These are really easy to make and packed with flavour from the fruit and nuts. They are quite high in calories, but much tastier and healthier than a chocolate bar. ♡

Makes 20
370 calories per flapjack
400 calories with chocolate drizzle

300g porridge oats
175g agave nectar
275g coconut oil
Finely grated zest and juice of
    1 large orange
2 tsp ground cinnamon
100g wholemeal plain flour
250g dates, finely chopped
75g sesame seeds
200g dried apricots, finely chopped
100g pistachios, roughly chopped
200g desiccated coconut

To finish (optional)
100g white chocolate, broken
    Into pieces

1   Preheat the oven to 180°C/Fan 160°C/Gas 4. Line a 20 x 30cm baking tin, at least 5cm deep, with baking parchment. Line a baking tray with parchment too.

2   Scatter the porridge oats on the lined baking tray and lightly toast in the oven for 10–15 minutes, tossing halfway through. Remove and set aside to cool.

3   Heat the agave nectar and coconut oil in a small saucepan over a low heat, stirring occasionally, until melted and smoothly combined. Take off the heat and stir in the orange zest and juice, and the cinnamon.

4   Put the toasted oats into a large bowl and add the flour, dates, sesame seeds, dried apricots, pistachios and desiccated coconut; mix well. Tip into the melted mixture and stir well to combine, making sure all the dry ingredients are coated in the oil and nectar mix.

5   Spoon the mixture into the prepared tin, pressing it down firmly. Bake for 25–30 minutes, until golden brown on top.

6   Remove from the oven and let cool for 5 minutes, then score into pieces with a sharp knife. Leave the flapjack to cool completely before lifting out of the tin.

7   For the topping, if using, melt the chocolate in a heatproof bowl over a pan of simmering water (check the base of the bowl isn't touching the water). Remove and let cool, then drizzle over the top of the flapjack.

8   Cut the flapjack into bars along the score lines. These flapjacks will keep in an airtight container in the fridge for up to a week.

Chocolate chip cookies

Quick and easy, these giant cookies are a sure-fire way to get children – or anyone – excited about cooking. They are made with wholemeal flour, which is better for you and also adds an extra nutty flavour, but I'm not claiming this makes them all that healthy! They're just a great way to encourage the family into the kitchen to get cooking. ♡ ❄

Makes 15
450 calories per cookie

220g butter, softened
150g light brown sugar
150g golden caster sugar
2 large free-range eggs
300g chocolate chips
1 tsp vanilla extract
1 tsp baking powder
1 tsp bicarbonate of soda
500g wholemeal plain flour
150g pecans or macadamia nuts,
    roughly chopped
A little flaky sea salt, for sprinkling

1 Preheat the oven to 180°C/Fan 160°C/Gas 4. Line two or three large baking trays with baking parchment.

2 Using an electric hand whisk, beat the butter and both sugars together in a large bowl, until light and creamy. Add the eggs one at a time, beating well after each addition.

3 Set aside a handful of chocolate chips to add later. Add the rest to the whisked mixture, along with the remaining ingredients (except the salt), and mix gently with a wooden spoon until it comes together to form a dough.

4 Divide the dough into 15 large pieces and roll into balls. Flatten each ball to a disc, about 7cm in diameter and 1cm thick. Place on the lined baking trays, leaving at least 5cm space in between the cookies. Sprinkle a few chocolate chips and salt flakes on top of each one.

5 Bake for 18–20 minutes or until the cookies are golden. Remove from the oven and leave to cool slightly on their trays before eating.

To freeze: Before baking, freeze the cookies in a single layer on trays (so they don't stick together as they freeze), then transfer to an airtight container. Bake from frozen, adding 2–3 minutes to the cooking time.

Coconut and raspberry loaf cake

We make a lot of loaf cakes at the pub because they are versatile when it comes to adding flavours, and are easy to portion into slices; they keep well too. Topped with a simple raspberry icing, fresh raspberries, coconut flakes and nuts, this cake looks really pretty, but the decoration doesn't need to be precise – just pile it all on top! ♡

10 slices
295 calories per slice

A little butter or oil, for greasing
2 ripe large bananas, peeled
    (250g peeled weight)
250ml coconut milk
1 vanilla pod, split and seeds
    scraped
150g golden caster sugar
    (or coconut sugar)
Finely grated zest and juice
    of 1 lemon
100g desiccated coconut
200g self-raising flour
1 tsp baking powder
300g raspberries

For the icing
120g icing sugar
About 1 tsp lemon juice

For the topping
10g coconut flakes, lightly toasted
50g hazelnuts, toasted and
    roughly chopped

1 Preheat the oven to 190°C/Fan 170°C/Gas 5. Grease a 900g (2lb) loaf tin and line the base and sides with baking parchment.

2 Mash the bananas in a large bowl, then add the coconut milk, vanilla seeds, sugar, lemon zest and juice and mix well. Add the desiccated coconut, flour and baking powder and mix to a smooth batter. Gently fold through half the raspberries.

3 Pour the mixture into the prepared loaf tin. Bake on the middle shelf of the oven for 35–40 minutes, until a skewer inserted into the middle comes out with just a few moist crumbs clinging. Remove from the oven and leave the cake in the tin for 5–10 minutes. Turn out onto a wire rack and leave to cool completely.

4 To make the icing, in a bowl, mash about eight of the remaining raspberries with a fork until smooth. Tip in the icing sugar and mix well, adding enough lemon juice to create a loose icing.

5 Drizzle the raspberry icing on top of the cake and scatter over the remaining fresh raspberries and the toasted coconut flakes and hazelnuts. This cake will keep for up to 3 days in a cake tin or other airtight container (without any fresh raspberries on top).

Orange, cardamom and polenta cake

Orange and cardamom is a classic pairing that works really well in a dessert if you prefer something a little less sweet. This is an elegant spin on an upside-down cake, and the polenta and almonds give a deliciously moist, dense texture. ♡

12 slices
405 calories per slice

**250g butter, softened, plus extra
    for greasing**
250g golden caster sugar
**1 vanilla pod, split and seeds
    scraped**
4 large free-range eggs
250g ground almonds
150g fine polenta
2 tsp baking powder
2 tsp ground cardamom
2 large oranges

For the orange syrup
**Juice from 2 oranges (ideally
    blood/blush oranges)**
1 tbsp honey
**3 tbsp orange liqueur, such as
    Grand Marnier**
4 tbsp water

To finish
30g pistachios, cut into fine slivers

1 Preheat the oven to 180°C/Fan 160°C/Gas 4. Grease a 23cm round springform cake tin and line with baking parchment.

2 Using an electric hand whisk, in a large bowl, beat together the butter, sugar and vanilla seeds until light and creamy. Beat in the eggs, one at a time, beating well after each addition.

3 In another bowl, mix together the ground almonds, polenta, baking powder and cardamom. Zest the 2 oranges over this dry mixture, then tip it into the whisked mixture and stir until well combined.

4 Peel the zested oranges, removing all of the white pith, then cut into slices. Lay the orange slices in the bottom of the prepared cake tin, overlapping them slightly and placing one slice in the middle. Carefully spoon the cake mixture into the tin.

5 Bake the cake on the middle shelf of the oven for 50–60 minutes, until the surface is light brown and the edge is coming away from the sides of the tin slightly. If it is getting too dark on top towards the end of the cooking time, cover loosely with foil. To check that it is cooked, insert a skewer into the centre; it should come out with just a few moist crumbs clinging. Remove from the oven and leave to cool in the tin for 10 minutes.

6 Turn the cake out onto a serving dish so that the oranges slices are now on the top. Carefully wave a cook's blowtorch over the surface of the cake, to lightly char the oranges slices. Leave to cool.

7 Meanwhile, for the syrup, put all the ingredients into a small saucepan and bring to the boil over a medium heat, stirring to combine. Lower the heat and simmer for about 10 minutes, until thickened slightly. Take off the heat and leave to cool for 15 minutes.

8 Brush the orange syrup over the surface of the cake to coat evenly. Sprinkle with the pistachios and cut into slices to serve. This cake will keep for up to 2 days in a cake tin or other airtight container.

Lemon and blueberry loaf cake

Lemon lends a delightful freshness to this moist loaf cake. It contrasts with the tangy sweetness of the blueberries, which soften and seep into the cake as they cook. ♡ ❄

10 slices
465 calories per slice

250g butter, softened, plus extra
    for greasing
200g golden caster sugar
4 large free-range eggs
100g Greek yoghurt (0% fat)
1 tbsp vanilla extract
2 tbsp lemon curd
Finely grated zest of 1 lemon
150g blueberries
250g self-raising flour
1 tsp baking powder

For the icing
175g icing sugar
1 tbsp plus 1 tsp Greek yoghurt
    (0% fat)
1 tbsp plus 1 tsp lemon curd

To decorate
100g blueberries
1 lemon, for zesting

1 Preheat the oven to 180°C/Fan 160°C/Gas 4. Grease a 900g (2lb) loaf tin and line with baking parchment.

2 Using an electric hand whisk, or a stand mixer fitted with the whisk attachment, beat the butter and sugar together until light and fluffy. Add the eggs, one at a time, beating after each addition.

3 Using a rubber spatula, fold the yoghurt, vanilla, lemon curd and lemon zest into the mixture. In another bowl, toss the blueberries with 2 tbsp of the flour.

4 Sift the remaining flour and baking powder over the cake mixture. Add the blueberries and fold in, using a large metal spoon, until just combined. Spoon the mixture into the loaf tin and gently level the surface.

5 Bake on the middle shelf of the oven for 45 minutes – 1 hour, until a skewer inserted into the middle comes out with just a few moist crumbs clinging. If the cake appears to be getting too brown in the oven, cover it loosely with foil. Remove from the oven and leave the cake in the tin for 5–10 minutes, then turn out onto a wire rack and leave to cool completely.

6 Once the cake has cooled, whisk the ingredients for the icing together until smooth. Spread the icing over the top of the cake. Decorate with blueberries and zest over the lemon. Cut into slices to serve.

To freeze: Wrap the whole un-iced cake in foil and seal in a plastic bag. Defrost at room temperature before icing. Or freeze individual iced slices, wrapped in foil; defrost at room temperature.

Chocolate beetroot cake

The rich flavours of dark chocolate work well with earthy ingredients like beetroot. The moist sponge is an amazing colour but it's all about the vibrant beetroot juice icing! ♡

12 slices
455 calories per slice

125ml sunflower oil, plus extra for greasing
300g dark chocolate (70% cocoa solids), broken into pieces
300g raw beetroot, peeled
4 large free-range eggs
200g light muscovado sugar
2 tsp vanilla extract
150g wholemeal self-raising flour
1 tsp baking powder
½ tsp ground cardamom

For the icing
250g icing sugar
About 2½ tbsp milk
Reserved beetroot juice (from above)

1 Preheat the oven to 180°C/Fan 160°C/Gas 4. Lightly oil a 23cm round springform cake tin and line with baking parchment.

2 Melt the chocolate in a heatproof bowl over a pan of simmering water, making sure the base of the bowl doesn't touch the water. Remove and leave to cool.

3 Coarsely grate the beetroot, then squeeze in your hands over a bowl, to extract (and save) the juice.

4 In a large bowl, beat the eggs, sugar, oil and vanilla extract together for 3–5 minutes, until thick and foamy. Sift the flour, baking powder and cardamom together over the mixture. Fold in gently until almost combined, then fold in the melted chocolate and grated beetroot.

5 Spoon the mixture into the prepared tin and spread gently to level. Bake on the middle oven shelf for 45 minutes, or until a skewer inserted into the centre comes out with just a few moist crumbs clinging.

6 For the icing, in a bowl, mix the icing sugar with enough milk and beetroot juice to make a thin, blush-pink icing. Save the rest of the beetroot juice.

7 Leave the cake in the tin for 10 minutes, then turn out onto a wire rack to cool. Lift onto a large plate, placing it upside down so you have a flat surface to ice.

8 Using a palette knife, spread the icing on top of the cake and let it drip over the edges. Dip a pastry brush into the remaining beetroot juice and flick it over the icing to create a random pattern. Slice the cake to serve. It will keep for 2 days in an airtight container.

Earl Grey fruit loaf

The addition of Earl Grey to this classic fruit loaf cake makes it a slice destined for an afternoon tea break. It travels and keeps well, so you could even take it to work with you, to resist a 4pm raid on the vending machine. ♡ ❄

10 slices
295 calories per slice

150g cold butter, diced, plus extra for greasing
2 Earl Grey tea bags
300ml just-boiled water
200g mixed dried fruit
100g dried figs, diced
60g dark muscovado sugar
275g self-raising flour
1 tsp ground mixed spice
1 tsp ground cinnamon
¼ tsp ground allspice
½ tsp sea salt
Finely grated zest of 1 orange
2 large free-range eggs, beaten

1   Preheat the oven to 180°C/Fan 160°C/Gas 4. Grease a 900g (2 lb) loaf tin and line it with baking parchment.

2   Place the tea bags in a medium saucepan and pour on the just-boiled water. Simmer for 2 minutes, then lift out and discard the tea bags. Add the dried fruit and sugar, stir and simmer for another 1 minute until the sugar is dissolved. Tip into a heatproof bowl and set aside to cool until just warm to the touch.

3   Put the flour into a large bowl, add the butter and rub in with your fingertips until the mixture resembles breadcrumbs. Add the ground spices, salt and orange zest and mix to combine. Make a well in the middle.

4   Stir the beaten eggs into the cooled tea mixture and pour into the dry ingredients. Stir until just combined then spoon into the prepared tin.

5   Bake on a lower oven shelf for about 50 minutes, until a skewer inserted into the middle comes out with just a few moist crumbs clinging. Remove from the oven and leave the cake in the tin for 5–10 minutes, then turn out onto a wire rack to cool a little more.

6   Slice and enjoy with a cuppa, ideally while still warm, though it's also nice at room temperature. It will keep for up to 3 days in a cake tin or other airtight container.

To freeze: Wrap the whole cake (or slices) in foil and seal in a plastic bag. Defrost at room temperature.

Banana choc ices

A more nutritious – and more delicious – alternative to shop-bought ice creams. If you have kids around, get them involved coating and dipping the choc ices into the nuts and dried raspberries to discover what their favourite toppings are. You will need eight mini ice-cream silicone moulds and eight wooden lolly sticks. ♡ ❄

3 medium-large bananas, peeled (350g peeled weight)
100g full-fat natural yoghurt
1 tbsp vanilla extract
100g good-quality dark chocolate (70% cocoa solids), broken into pieces
2 tbsp coconut oil

For the toppings
Mixed nuts, toasted and finely chopped
Coconut flakes, toasted and lightly crushed
Pistachio nuts, finely chopped
Freeze-dried raspberries

1 Put the bananas, yoghurt and vanilla extract into a food processor and blend until smooth. Pour the mixture into 8 mini ice-cream silicone moulds. Insert a lolly stick into each one and place in the freezer for at least 3 hours until frozen solid.

2 When the lollies are frozen, place the chocolate and coconut oil in a small heatproof bowl over a pan of simmering water; make sure the base of the bowl isn't touching the water. Stir over a low heat until melted. Remove from the heat and leave until cool to the touch, but still runny.

3 Line a tray with baking parchment or a non-stick silicone mat. Take the banana lollies from the freezer.

4 Working quickly, dip one lolly at a time into the melted chocolate and turn to coat all over. Lift out and sprinkle with your choice of topping. Place on the prepared tray; the chocolate will set almost instantly. Repeat with the remaining ice lollies. Eat straight away or return to the freezer until you're ready to serve.

TIP ✔ If you are freezing these after assembling, wrap each one loosely in baking parchment then place in a freezerproof container in the freezer until ready to eat.

GLUTEN-FREE

These recipes don't contain any gluten, though you may need to leave out an 'optional ingredient' such as flatbread. Watch out for hidden gluten: when you're buying grains like rice, oats and polenta, check that the packet says they're guaranteed gluten-free or else they might contain traces of it. The same goes for sauces, condiments, stock cubes and baking powder.

DAIRY-FREE

These recipes are all dairy-free. Leave out any 'optional' serving suggestions that have dairy, such as raita or Parmesan. And if the recipe gives the choice of using a dairy-free ingredient (for greasing a tin maybe), go for that option!

INDEX

Thanks

Right, let's kick this off... as it's a family book, none of this would be possible without the huge support I get from my own family. Beth, you're just amazing. Thank you for putting little man to bed and getting him up when I'm not there, because I'm too busy doing stuff like this! Acey, you're just the greatest thing ever! I'm so pleased that you like just a little bit of this food before you decide to spit it out and would rather have chippies. You guys really are the best and are the whole point in doing all of this. Waiting in the wings as the pit crew, Suze and Katie, thank you so much for being ever reliable.

Huge shout out to Alex Longstaff, yet again you've helped me focus (a little bit, as I'm right now staring out of the window watching a flash car go by, but you know what, you do try your best!). Your help is invaluable and thank you for your patience.

To everybody at Absolute and Bloomsbury – Nigel Newton, Jon Croft, Xa Shaw Stewart, Richard Atkinson, Natalie Bellos, Amanda Shipp, Jen Hampson, Ellen Williams, Becky Anderson and Marina Asenjo – thank you guys so much for making, printing, publishing, trusting and believing in another brilliant book that gets people off their bums and into the kitchen cooking. Your ongoing support is so valuable and hugely appreciated. Can't wait to see where we decide to go for lunch this year, Nigel!

To the Marlow pirates. Everybody at The Hand and Flowers, The Coach and The Butcher's Tap. You guys keep those pirate ships steady while I'm trying to navigate! Love you guys so much, I'm so proud of all of you. Such exceptional work with constant high standards, love you all very, very much.

For those pirate ship deserters who have found their way to the big smoke – what an incredibly exciting year! You guys really are smashing it with an amazing project. Keep driving forward, Kerridge's Bar & Grill crew!

To Janet Illsley for skilfully editing all the words so they fit the pages, and to designer David Eldridge at Two Associates for making the pages ping and look absolutely stunning, thank you so much. It really is a joy working with you guys.

Recipe testing and helping find the right words to say – Laura Herring, thank you so much for not making my mouth say daft things! Or even if it did, making it sound better than the actual words! Jenna Leiter and Esther Clark, I hope you enjoyed eating plenty of those tested recipes! Thank you Jen Hopley and Dr Rachel Allen for recipe analysis and nutritional consultancy – you've both been amazing.

Thank you so much to Georgia Glynn Smith for the use of your beautiful house to help this book feel real. It's an amazing family home you have and we were all so very pleased to spend time in it.

Massive shout out and thank you to the guys who really do sit on the front line of this book and create the content. Food styling – Chris Mackett, Holly Cochrane, Rosie Mackean and Alice Ostan. You guys worked tirelessly, constantly creating beautiful food! And of course, a massive thank you, heartfelt love, hugs, fist bumps and high fives to you, Nicole Herft. You are just such a vibrant, massive lover of food and life and your energy levels are infectious. You bring so much to this book and to my life, and we love you dearly. Thank you so much.

Huge thank you once again to the brilliant art director Lydia McPherson for styling, creating and driving forward this great bit of photography, which you should be so proud of, because I certainly am!

I've always thought that a book isn't a book without pictures in it, which is where the immensely talented, ever-dependable and super-lovely Cristian Barnett comes in. Thank you so much once again for capturing every moment at the right time. Energy, heart and soul and a sense of place show through on these pages. Chief, you are the greatest. And behind every great man, there needs to a super trusty sidekick – Bríd Ní Luasaigh, thank you for helping make Cristian look so good, ha ha!

To the whole team at Bone Soup, who helped take people on their journey by encouraging them to cook, and helped to choose recipes that are not only inspirational but also achievable. Most importantly, you've created and delivered a brilliant television show. Massive thank you to Richard Bowron, Sarah Myland, Hannah Corneck, Georgia Mills, Sophie Wells, Richard Hill, Jack Coathupe, Robbie Johnson, Nick Murray, Tom Berrow, Dan Berrow, Joanna Boyle, Susie Millns, Dominic Fearon, Lucy Kattenhorn, Chris Mallett, Chris White, Lizzie Minnion, Richard Lambert and Tony Osborne.

A big thank you to the BBC, David Brindley and Michael Jochnowitz for once again believing in us and letting a bloke with a bumpkin accent appear on the telly!

To the two guiding lights who keep an eye on the daft things that I say and make sure I do nothing too untoward – Borra Garson and Gemma Bell, thank you so much for your support. I think we've had a pretty good year – I haven't done anything too stupid!

Lastly, to all the brilliant families who have taken part in the show: I'm so proud of all of you for changing the way that you look at, buy and eat food. The difference you made is an inspiration to everybody who is going to be buying and reading this book. Thank you all very, very much!

BLOOMSBURY ABSOLUTE

Bloomsbury Publishing Plc

50 Bedford Square, London, WC1B 3DP, UK

BLOOMSBURY, BLOOMSBURY ABSOLUTE,
the Diana logo and the Absolute Press logo
are trademarks of Bloomsbury Publishing Plc

First published in Great Britain 2018

The information contained in this book is
provided by way of general guidance in
relation to the specific subject matters
addressed herein, but it is not a substitute
for specialist dietary advice. It should not
be relied on for medical, pharmaceutical,
healthcare or other professional advice on
specific dietary or health needs. This book is
sold with the understanding that the author
and publisher are not engaged in rendering
medical, health or any other kind of personal
or professional services. The reader should
consult a competent medical or health
professional before adopting any of the
suggestions in this book or drawing any
inferences from it

The author and publisher specifically disclaim,
as far as the law allows, any responsibility from
any liability, loss or risk (personal or otherwise)
which is incurred as a consequence, directly
or indirectly, of the use and applications of
any of the contents of this book

If you are on medication of any description,
please consult your doctor or other health
professional before embarking on any fast
or diet

A catalogue record for this book is available
from the British Library

ISBN: HB: 978-1-4729-6280-5

10 9 8 7 6 5 4 3 2 1

Project Editor: Janet Illsley

Design: Two Associates

Photographs: Cristian Barnett,
    crisbarnett.com

Food Styling: Tom Kerridge and Nicole Herft

Art Direction and Styling: Lydia McPherson

Illustrations: Two Associates

Index: Hilary Bird

Printed and bound in Germany by Mohn Media

FSC
www.fsc.org
MIX
Paper from
responsible sources
FSC® C011124

To find out more about our authors and books
visit www.bloomsbury.com and sign up for our
newsletters